Investigative Maths

Developing children's investigative and thinking skills in the Daily Maths Lesson

Year 6

Peter Clarke

William Collins' dream of knowledge for all began with the publication of his first book in 1819. A self-educated mill worker, he not only enriched millions of lives, but also founded a flourishing publishing house. Today, staying true to this spirit, Collins books are packed with inspiration, innovation and practical expertise. They place you at the centre of a world of possibility and give you exactly what you need to explore it.

Collins. Do more.

Published by Collins
An imprint of HarperCollins*Publishers*
77–85 Fulham Palace Road
Hammersmith
London
W6 8JB

Browse the complete Collins catalogue at
www.collinseducation.com

© HarperCollins*Publishers* Limited 2005

10 9 8 7 6 5 4 3 2 1

ISBN 0 00 719476 5

Peter Clarke asserts his moral right to be identified as the author of this work

British Library Cataloguing in Publication Data
A Catalogue record for this publication is available from the British Library

Publishing Manager: Melanie Hoffman
Project Editor: Natasha Reid
Editor: Jean Rustean
Cover design by Susi Martin
Cover illustration by Gary Dunn
Series design by Neil Adams
Illustrations by Juliet Breese

Printed and bound by Martins the Printers, Berwick on Tweed

Contents

Introduction

Mathematical problem solving encompasses both using and applying mathematics to the solution of problems arising from the environment and reasoning and investigating questions that have arisen from within mathematics itself.

Being able to use mathematics to analyse situations and solve real-life problems is a major reason for studying the subject. Frequent use of everyday experiences will give meaning to the children's mathematical experiences. Children need to be able to apply the mathematics they have learned to real-life situations in their environment. They also need to be able to interpret and make meaning from their results. Teachers should structure situations in which children investigate problems relevant to their daily lives and relating to the recent mathematical knowledge, skills and understanding the children have acquired.

Studies of effective teachers of numeracy (Askew *et al.* 1997) have found that the most effective teachers have a 'connectionist' orientation to the teaching of mathematics. These teachers encourage children to think and talk about what they are doing and to make connections between different areas and aspects of the subject.

Investigative Maths is a series of six books for Year 1 to Year 6. It is designed to assist children to practise and consolidate the three strands of the Mathematics National Curriculum Attainment Target 1 – Using and applying mathematics: problem solving, communicating and reasoning; as well as the problem solving strand of the National Numeracy Strategy (NNS) *Framework for teaching mathematics R – 6*. At the same time other key mathematical strands are also developed such as numbers and the number system, calculations, and measures, shape and space.

Investigative Maths aims to provide teachers with a resource that enables children to:
- use and apply mathematics to solve problems arising from the environment
- reason and investigate questions that have arisen from within mathematics itself
- practise their pure mathematical knowledge and skills in an applied context
- apply their mathematical problem solving skills in contexts that are topical, relevant and meaningful

The activities

Investigative Maths contains two different types of activities:

Everyday problem solving

These activities include problems arising from the environment.

The activities in this section have been organised into themes. There are 12 themes, each with four different activities. The four activities can either be used together in one lesson, with different groups working on different activities, or individually over the course of a week or more.

When children solve everyday problems:
- the purpose and meaning is clear
- it is motivating
- it allows them to take control of the mathematics, choosing methods that suit them

- they are likely to feel confident about multi-tasking
- the context provides many clues and stimuli to support their thinking
- the mathematics is practical rather than abstract, and builds more obviously on children's previous experiences

Mathematical problem solving

These activities include problems arising from within mathematics itself.

When children solve mathematical problems they:

- use prior mathematical knowledge to acquire new mathematical knowledge
- make connections

Resources

- Almost all the activities in *Investigative Maths* suggest that pencil and paper be given to the children. This allows the children to feel free to work out the answers and record their thinking in ways that are appropriate to them. Giving children a large sheet of paper, such as A1, provides them with an excellent prompt to use when discussing their work, especially during the plenary. It also aids assessment for children's problem solving, communicating and reasoning skills.
- An important problem solving skill is to be able to identify not only the mathematics, but also what equipment to use. For this reason many of the activities do not name the specific resources that are needed. For example, in problems involving measures, the resources section states simply 'measuring equipment' to make teachers aware that a range of measuring equipment will need to be on hand for the children to choose.
- In most activities calculators have not been listed under the resources section so that children have to decide for themselves the most appropriate way of calculating.
- Teachers also need to be aware that some of the activities require them or the children to bring in to school resources from home.

Answers

- In the *Mathematical problem solving* section, answers are given to the primary activities where necessary, not to the extensions .
- In the *Everyday problem solving* section, no answers are given.

Investigative Maths and the daily mathematics lesson

The activities contained in *Investigative Maths* are ideally suited to the daily mathematics lesson. They can be used to:

- introduce new mathematical concepts using a discovery approach to teaching and learning
- consolidate children's understanding of previously taught mathematical concepts
- provide an opportunity for children to use and apply their 'pure' mathematical knowledge in more applied, problem solving and investigative contexts

- extend the more able pupils
- challenge the 'quick finishers'

Although the activities are designed to be used by individuals, pairs or groups of children, they will be enhanced greatly if children are able to work together in pairs or groups. By working collaboratively, children are more likely to develop their problem solving, communicating and reasoning skills.

Problem solving skills

Investigative Maths aims to develop in children the key skills required to tackle and solve mathematical investigations.

These include:
- reading and making sense of a problem
- recognising key words, relevant information and redundant information
- finding parts of a problem that can be tackled
- recognising the mathematics which can be used to help solve a problem
- deciding which number operation(s) to perform and in which order
- choosing an efficient way of calculating
- presenting information and results in a clear and organised way
- changing measurements to the same units before calculating
- getting into the habit of checking for themselves whether the answer makes sense

Thinking skills

The National Curriculum (2000) outlines the thinking skills that complement the key knowledge, skills and understanding which are embedded in the primary curriculum.

Investigative Maths aims to develop in children these key thinking skills.

Information – processing skills
- locate, collect relevant information
- sort, classify, sequence, compare and analyse part and/or whole relationships

Reasoning skills
- give reasons for opinions and actions
- draw inferences and make deductions
- use precise language to explain what they think
- make judgements and decisions informed by reason or evidence

Enquiry skills
- ask relevant questions
- pose and define problems
- plan what to do and how to research
- predict outcomes and anticipate conclusions
- test conclusions and improve ideas

Creative thinking skills
- generate and extend ideas
- suggest hypotheses

- apply imagination
- look for alternative innovative outcomes

Evaluative skills
- evaluate information
- judge the value of what they read, hear or do
- develop criteria for judging the value of their own and others' work or ideas
- have confidence in their judgement

Problem solving strategies

If children are actively to engage in mathematical investigations they must be taught appropriate problem solving strategies.

Children need to be taught to:
- look for a pattern or sequence
- experiment or act out a problem
- make a drawing or model
- make a list, table or chart
- write a number sentence
- see mathematical connections
- make and test a prediction
- make a generalisation
- establish a proof
- account for all known possibilities
- solve a simpler related problem
- work backwards

A model for mathematical investigations

To be successful at solving mathematical investigations, children need to:
- be given ample opportunities to practise problem solving skills and strategies
- work systematically and co-operatively
- use what knowledge and skills they have to help acquire new knowledge and skills
- develop self monitoring and self assessment
- talk about their work and reflect on their thinking

The model on page 8 provides children with a systematic approach to solving mathematical investigations. It also enables children to practise and develop their thinking skills.

Photocopy and enlarge this page, make it into a poster, and display it for all the class to see and follow.

Children need to be taught to use this model flexibly. They must realise that:
- not all eight stages of the model are required for every investigation
- the amount of time that is spent on each of the eight stages depends upon the nature of the investigation
- any stage in the model can be revisited at any time

A model for mathematical investigations

Recognise
What is the problem?

Reflect
What have I learned from this?

Use
What do I already know that can help me solve this problem?

Share
Let's tell others.

Support
What do I need to find out and use to help me solve this problem?

Check and assess
- Am I correct?
- How well did I do?

Decide and try
- How might I go about solving this problem?
- What is the best way?
- Let's try.

Review
Is it working?
Yes – Let's continue.
No – Let's go back.

Investigative Maths (Y6) © Harper*Collins*Publishers Ltd 2005

Curriculum information

The activities in *Investigative Maths* are designed to improve children's attainment in the three strands of the National Curriculum Attainment Target 1 – Using and applying mathematics.

In *problem solving* by:
- using a range of problem solving strategies
- trying different approaches to a problem
- applying mathematics in a new context
- checking their results

In *communicating* by:
- interpreting information
- recording information systematically
- using mathematical language, symbols, notation and diagrams correctly and precisely
- presenting and interpreting methods, solutions and conclusions in the context of the problem

In *reasoning* by:
- giving clear explanations of their methods and reasoning
- investigating and making general statements
- recognising patterns in their results
- making use of a wider range of evidence to justify results through logical reasoned argument
- drawing their own conclusions

The activities also provide children with an opportunity to practise and consolidate the following Year 6 solving problems objectives from the NNS *Framework*:

Topic: *Making decisions*
- Choose and use appropriate number operations to solve problems, and appropriate ways of calculating: mental, mental with jottings, written methods, calculator.

Topic: *Reasoning and generalising about numbers or shapes*
- Explain methods and reasoning, orally and in writing.
- Solve mathematical problems or puzzles, recognise and explain patterns and relationships, generalise and predict. Suggest extensions by asking 'What if…?'
- Make and investigate a general statement about familiar numbers or shapes by finding examples that satisfy it.
- Develop from explaining a generalised relationship in words to expressing it in a formula using letters as symbols.

Topic: *Problems involving 'real life', money and measures*
- Identify and use appropriate operations (including combinations of operations) to solve word problems involving numbers and quantities based on 'real life', money or measures (including time), using one or more steps, including converting pounds to foreign currency, or vice versa, and calculating percentages such as VAT.
- Explain methods and reasoning.

In addition to these objectives, the charts on pages 10 and 11 show which other strand(s) and topic(s) each of the activities covers.

Everyday problem solving

These activities include problems arising from the environment.

Page	Activity	Theme	Title	Place value, ordering and rounding	Properties of numbers and number sequences	Fractions, decimals, percentages, ratio and proportion	Addition	Subtraction	Multiplication	Division	Money	Organising and interpreting data	Measures: Length (L), Mass (M), Capacity (C), Time (T), Area (A), Perimeter (P)	Shape and space
14	1a	Ideal bedroom	Floor plan										●L	●
14	1b		Cost of furniture				●		●		●		●L	
15	1c		Decorating				●		●		●		●L,A,P	
15	1d		Your own bedroom				●	●	●		●		●L,A,P	
16	2a	Money matters	Earning interest			●			●	●	●			
16	2b		Value of cars			●		●	●	●	●	●		
17	2c		House prices				●	●	●	●	●	●		
17	2d		Cost of living				●	●	●	●	●			
18	3a	Fibonacci numbers	The Fibonacci sequence		●		●					●		
18	3b		Fibonacci totals		●		●					●		
19	3c		Consecutive Fibonacci numbers	●	●				●	●		●		
19	3d		Fibonacci digits	●	●							●		
20	4a	Pascal's triangle	Pascal's pattern		●		●					●		
20	4b		Pascal's powers		●		●		●			●		
21	4c		Pascal and …		●		●					●		
21	4d		Dividing Pascal's triangle		●		●	●	●	●		●		
22	5a	Our solar system	Distance from the Sun				●	●				●	●L	
22	5b		Hours a day			●			●	●		●	●T	
23	5c		Orbiting the Sun						●	●		●	●T	
23	5d		Speeding planets						●	●			●L,T	
24	6a	Entertainment	24 frames per second						●	●		●	●T	
24	6b		West End theatre						●	●	●	●		
25	6c		Favourite 10 books									●		
25	6d		Music			●						●		
26	7a	Patterns	Square grid pattern										●L	●
26	7b		Co-ordinates pattern										●L	●
27	7c		Circular pattern						●				●L	●
27	7d		Shape pattern						●				●L	●
28	8a	A to Z	Letter frequency	●								●		
28	8b		Different languages									●		
29	8c		Scrabble			●						●		
29	8d		Morse code									●		
30	9a	Flying	Cost per kilometre					●		●	●		●L	
30	9b		Boeing 737							●			●M	
31	9c		Flying speed					●	●	●			●L	
31	9d		How far can they fly?					●	●	●			●L,C	
32	10a	Energy	Cost of light			●		●	●		●			
32	10b		Solar power			●			●	●	●			
33	10c		Travel and trees			●	●	●	●	●	●			
33	10d		Battery power			●		●	●	●	●			
34	11a	The Developing World	Fair trade					●	●	●	●			
34	11b		Who gets what?				●	●	●	●	●	●		
35	11c		How many pairs of jeans?					●	●	●	●			
35	11d		Charities				●	●	●	●	●			
36	12a	Town planning	Planning Newtown				●	●	●	●			●L	●
36	12b		Redesigning your school				●	●	●	●			●L,A,P	
37	12c		Designing a housing estate			●		●	●	●			●L,A,P	●
37	12d		New school sports centre				●	●	●	●			●L,A,P	●

Mathematical problem solving

These activities include problems arising from within mathematics itself.

Page	Activity	Title	Place value, ordering and rounding	Properties of numbers and number sequences	Fractions, decimals, percentages, ratio and proportion	Addition	Subtraction	Multiplication	Division	Money	Organising and interpreting data	Measures: Length (L), Mass (M), Capacity (C), Time (T), Area (A), Perimeter (P)	Shape and space
38	13	Multiply, divide and round	●		●			●	●		●		
38	14	Making zero	●			●	●				●		
39	15	Adding consecutive numbers		●		●					●		
39	16	Square numbers		●				●					
40	17	Powers		●				●					
40	18	Triangular numbers		●		●	●				●		
41	19	Proper factors		●				●	●		●		
41	20	Prime numbers		●				●	●		●		
42	21	Consecutive prime numbers		●		●		●	●		●		
42	22	Prime factors		●				●	●		●		
43	23	LCM × GCF = ?		●				●	●				
43	24	Nearer to 1			●	●	●						
44	25	Unitary fractions			●	●	●						
44	26	Fractions and decimals			●						●		
45	27	Percentages			●			●	●				
45	28	Dominoes			●	●	●	●	●				
46	29	Making even numbers		●		●	●				●		
46	30	Between 200 and 300	●		●	●	●	●	●				
47	31	Decimal calculation patterns			●	●	●				●		
47	32	Letter calculations				●	●				●		
48	33	Number puzzles				●	●	●	●		●		
48	34	Making magic squares				●	●				●		
49	35	Interesting decimals			●	●	●						
49	36	Multiplication pairs						●			●		
50	37	Multiplication cards	●					●					
50	38	Dice calculations	●					●	●				
51	39	Algebraic expressions	●			●	●	●			●		
51	40	Adding squares		●		●		●					
52	41	Consecutive odd numbers		●		●	●		●		●		
52	42	1, 2, 5 and 8				●	●	●	●		●		
53	43	Currency calculator						●	●	●	●		
53	44	VAT						●	●	●			
54	45	Coins worth			●			●	●		●		
54	46	Where are they?									●		
55	47	Sorting cards									●		
55	48	Handling dice data				●	●	●	●		●		
56	49	Metric and imperial measures			●			●			●	● L,M,C	
56	50	Temperature			●	●	●	●				● Temp	
57	51	Dan's van				●	●	●	●			● L,M	
57	52	Time differences				●	●					● T	
58	53	Field measurements				●		●				● A,P	
58	54	Triangular areas						●	●			● A	●
59	55	Area of a circle	●					●				● A	●
59	56	Polygon designs											●
60	57	Translating shapes											●
60	58	Reflect, translate, rotate											●
61	59	Co-ordinating shapes											●
61	60	Angle shapes				●	●	●					●

Assessment and record keeping

Investigative Maths activities may be used with the whole class or with groups of children as an assessment activity. Linked to the topic that is being studied at present, *Investigative Maths* will provide you with an indication of how well the children have understood the objectives being covered as well as their problem solving skills.

The Assessment and record keeping format on page 13 can be used to assess and level children in Attainment Target 1: Using and applying mathematics. By observing individual children while they undertake an *Investigative Maths* activity, discussing their work with them, and subsequently marking their work, you will be able to gain a good understanding of their problem solving, communicating and reasoning skills.

Your judgements about an individual child's abilities should also take into account:

- mastery of other objectives from the 'Solving problems' strand of the NNS *Framework*
- performance in whole class discussions
- participation in group work
- work presented in exercise books
- any other written evidence

Once you have decided which level 'best fits' a particular child write the child's name in the box under the appropriate level. You may wish to identify how competent a child is at that level by using the following key:

C – Becoming competent in most criteria at this level

B – Competent in most criteria at this level

A – Very competent in most criteria at this level

It is envisaged that one copy of the Assessment and record keeping format would be used for your entire class.

Attainment Target 1: Using and applying mathematics
Assessment and record keeping format

Year: _____ Class: _____

Teacher: _____

LEVEL 3

Problem solving	Communicating	Reasoning	
• Develop different mathematical approaches to a problem. • Look for ways to overcome difficulties. • Begin to make decisions and realise that results may vary according to the 'rule' used. • Begin to organise work. • Check results.	• Discuss mathematical work. • Begin to explain thinking. • Use and interpret mathematical symbols and diagrams.	• Understand a general statement. • Investigate general statements and predictions by finding and trying out examples.	

LEVEL 4

Problem solving	Communicating	Reasoning	
• Develop own strategies for solving problems. • Use own strategies for working within mathematics. • Use own strategies for applying mathematics to practical contexts.	• Present information and results in a clear and organised way.	• Search for solutions by trying out own ideas.	

LEVEL 5

Problem solving	Communicating	Reasoning	
• Identify and obtain necessary information. • Check results, considering whether these are sensible.	• Show understanding of situations by describing them mathematically using symbols, words and diagrams.	• Draw simple conclusions. • Give an explanation for their reasoning.	

LEVEL 6

Problem solving	Communicating	Reasoning	
• Carry through substantial tasks. • Solve complex problems by independently breaking them down into smaller, more manageable tasks.	• Interpret, discuss and synthesise information presented in a variety of mathematical forms. • Use writing to explain and inform diagrams.	• Begin to give mathematical justifications.	

GENERAL COMMENTS

Investigative Maths (Y6) © HarperCollins*Publishers* Ltd 2005

1a Floor plan

• furniture catalogues
• squared paper
• ruler
• pencil and paper

- Draw to scale a floor plan of your ideal bedroom.

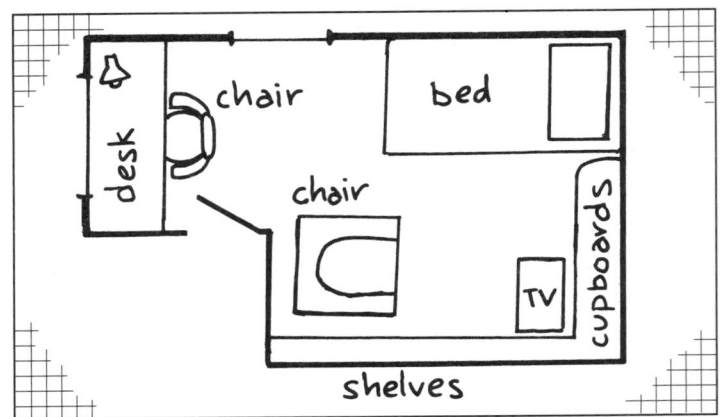

- Include all of the furniture to scale.
- Write all the dimensions on your plan, including the furniture.
- Don't forget windows and doors.

1b Cost of furniture

• furniture catalogues
• pencil and paper

- Choose the furniture you would like for your ideal bedroom.
- How much would this all cost?

- Make sure that the things you choose will fit into your ideal bedroom.

1c Decorating

• decorating catalogues
• pencil and paper

- Investigate the cost of decorating your ideal bedroom.

- Are you going to use paint or wallpaper? How many tins of paint or how many rolls of wallpaper will you need?
- Don't forget the ceiling and floor.

1d Your own bedroom

• furniture and decorating catalogues
• measuring equipment
• pencil and paper

- Imagine you have a budget of £300 to spend to make your own bedroom more like your ideal bedroom. What are you doing to do?

- Are you going to change the furniture in your bedroom? If so, make sure it fits.
- What about redecorating the walls, ceiling and floor?
- Do you have any money left over? How much?

2a Earning interest

- financial section from newspapers
- pencil and paper

- Investigate the best rate of interest you could earn if you had £100 to invest.

- If you left the money there for 5 years, including the interest, how much money would you have at the end of 5 years?

- Remember that each time you are paid interest it will start earning interest as well.

2b Value of cars

- used car magazines
- pencil and paper

- Choose a type of car you would like. It can cost no more than £30 000!

- Investigate how much it loses value each year as it gets older.

- Compare this to the following three cars:
  - Volkswagen Golf
  - Ford Focus
  - Honda Civic.

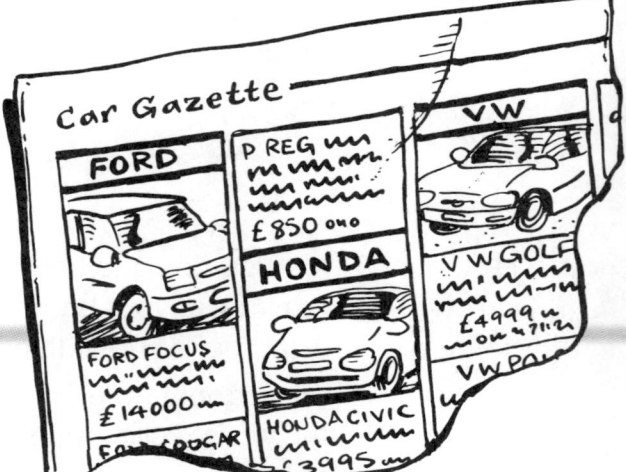

- Think about how you are going to measure this.
  As a percentage? In pounds?

- How are you going to show your results?

2c House prices

- property section from newspapers
- pencil and paper

- What is the cost of an average house in your local area?
- How does this compare with prices 1 / 2 / 3 / …10 years ago?
- Investigate the rise and fall of house prices in your local area over the past 10 years.
- How does this compare with prices in other parts of the country?
- Is this the same for flats?

- Think about how you are going to display your results.

2d Cost of living

- pencil and paper

- Investigate how much money a family of five, of two adults and three children, need to live for a month.

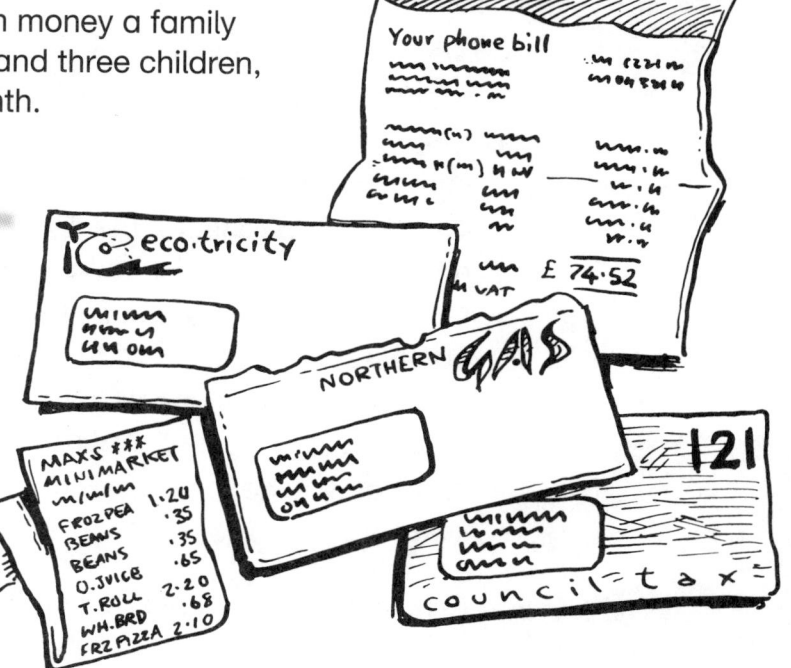

- Think about:
  - rent / mortgage
  - gas
  - electricity
  - telephone
  - food
  - other expenses.

- pencil and paper

3a The Fibonacci sequence

A man called Fibonacci studied the natural world and noticed a pattern in the number of things such as petals on flowers and leaves on stems.

- The sequence starts: 1, 1, 2, 3, 5, 8, 13, 21, 34, 55...
- Describe the pattern.
- Work out what the next five numbers in the sequence are.

- What if you started with a number other than 1?

- pencil and paper

3b Fibonacci totals

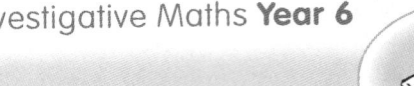

- Starting at 1, write the first 20 numbers in the Fibonacci sequence.
- Add together the first 5 Fibonacci numbers. Write down the number.
- Now add together the first 6 Fibonacci numbers and write down the number.
- This time add together the first 7 Fibonacci numbers and write down the number.
- Finally, add together the first 8 Fibonacci numbers and write down the number.
- Look at the four numbers you have just written down. Compare these with the numbers of the Fibonacci sequence.
- What do you notice?

- Can you predict what the sum of the first 9 / 10 / 11 ... Fibonacci numbers are?

3c Consecutive Fibonacci numbers

- pencil and paper

- Starting at 1, write the first 20 numbers in the Fibonacci sequence.
- Choose four consecutive Fibonacci numbers.
- Find the products of the first and last numbers, and the second and third numbers.
- Now work out the difference between the two products.
- Choose four more consecutive Fibonacci numbers and repeat the above.
- What do you notice?
- What if you started with a number other than 1?

- Choose three consecutive Fibonacci numbers.
- Multiply the first and last numbers together, and square the second number.
- Now work out the difference between the two products.
- Choose three more consecutive Fibonacci numbers and repeat the above.
- What do you notice?
- What if you started with a number other than 1?

3d Fibonacci digits

- pencil and paper

- Starting at 1, write the first 20 numbers in the Fibonacci sequence.
- Write the units digits of all the numbers.
- What patterns do you notice?
- What if you started with a number other than 1?

- What other patterns can you discover in the Fibonacci sequence?

4a Pascal's pattern

• pencil and paper

This triangular pattern of numbers was discovered in 1653 by a French mathematician named Blaise Pascal.

```
            1
          1   1
        1   2   1
      1   3   3   1
    1   4   6   4   1
  1   5   10   10   5   1
```

- What is the pattern?
- Write the next two lines of the pattern at the base of the triangle.

- What other patterns do you notice?

4b Pascal's powers

• pencil and paper

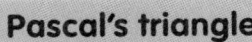

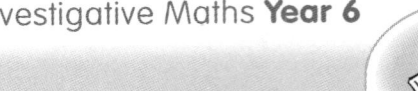

A 'power' tells us how many of the same number are multiplied together. 6×6 is shortened to 6^2, where 2 is the power. We say it as '6 to the power of 2' or '6 squared'. $6 \times 6 \times 6$ is shortened to 6^3, where 3 is the power. We say it as '6 to the power of 3'.

$$6^2 = 6 \times 6 = 36$$
$$6^3 = 6 \times 6 \times 6 = 216$$

- Investigate the link between the sum of each row in Pascal's triangle and 2 and its powers.

```
          1
        1   1
      1   2   1
    1   3   3   1
  1   4   6   4   1
```

- Can you predict what the sum of row 10 / 11 / 12 … 20 is?

4c   Pascal and ...

- pencil and paper

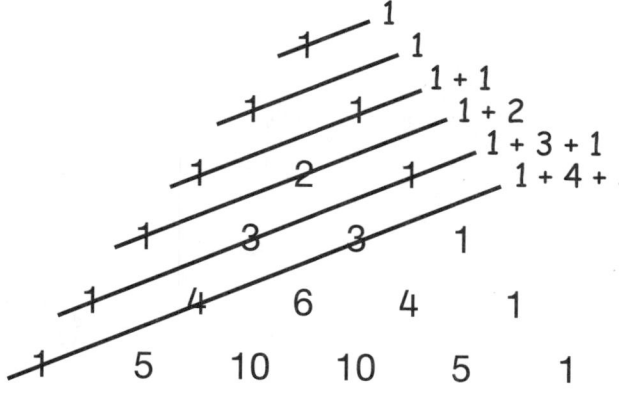

- Investigate the sum of the diagonals in Pascal's triangle.
- What pattern do you notice?

- Investigate the link between Pascal's triangle and triangular numbers.

4d   Dividing Pascal's triangle

- coloured pencils
- pencil and paper

- When you divide a number by 2, the remainder is 0 or 1.
- Colour each number in Pascal's triangle according to its remainder.
- What pattern do you notice?
- Can you explain it?

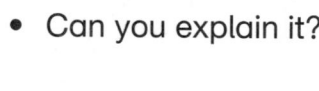

- When you divide a number by 3, the remainder is 0, 1, or 2. Divide the numbers in Pascal's triangle by 3 and colour them according to their remainder. Can you explain the pattern?
- What about the patterns you get when you divide by other numbers?

5a Distance from the Sun

- Investigate the distances of all the planets in our solar system from the Sun.
- Calculate how far each planet is from its nearest neighbour.

- Which two planets are the closest together?

5b Hours a day

One day on Earth lasts 24 hours.

- Approximately what percentage of your day is spent at school?
- How many hours would you spend at school each day if you lived on each of the other planets, assuming you spent the same percentage of the day at school?

Planet	Mercury	Venus	Earth	Mars	Jupiter	Saturn	Uranus	Neptune	Pluto
hours in 1 day	58·646	243·01	24	24·62	9·84	10·23	17·24	16·11	153·288

- How long would you spend asleep on each of the planets each day?

5c Orbiting the Sun

The Earth takes one year to orbit the Sun.

Jupiter takes about 12 years to orbit the Sun.

- Investigate how long each of the other planets takes to orbit the Sun.

Someone who is 12 years old on Earth would be 1 year old on Jupiter.

- Approximately how old would you be on each of the other planets in our solar system?

5d Speeding planets

The Earth orbits the Sun. It travels a distance of 107 292 km each hour.

- Calculate how far the Earth travels in:
  - the time it takes you to walk across the classroom
  - a maths lesson
  - a school day.

It takes one year for the Earth to orbit the Sun.

- Approximately how many millions of kilometres does the Earth travel in one year?

Mercury is the fastest travelling planet. It travels a distance of 172 318 km each hour.

- How much further does Mercury travel than the Earth in 24 hours?

6a 24 frames per second

- entertainment section of a newspaper
- videos
- pencil and paper

Films consist of many separate images called frames, lined up in a row. Each frame is slightly different. For example, one frame might show a football. The next frame might show the football being kicked. When these frames are played together, we see the motion of the ball being kicked.

24 frames are needed to make one second of film. This is known as '24 frames per second'.

- Investigate the number of frames needed to make an average length film.

- Investigate the length of your favourite films and the number of frames needed.

6b West End theatre

- entertainment section of a newspaper
- pencil and paper

The West End in central London is the heart of the theatre district.

- Compare the prices of different West End shows.
- What is the mode, range, median and mean of West End theatre prices?

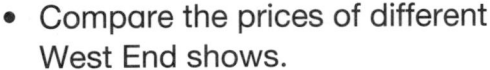

- Think about:
  – how many different shows you are going to choose to make your comparisons
  – how you are going to choose which shows to compare
  – how you are going to find out the prices
  – what the average seat price is in each theatre.

6c Favourite 10 books

- pencil and paper

- Investigate the 10 favourite books in your school.

- How are you going to display your results?

6d Music

- pencil and paper

- Investigate how children in your school listen to music.
- What percentage of children access music in each of the different ways?
- If some use several ways, which is their favourite? Why?

- Think about:
  CD   MP3 player   Radio   Television   Internet
- How are you going to display your results?

7a Square grid pattern

- squared paper
- ruler
- pencil

- Draw this grid on squared paper.
- Join 1 to 10, 2 to 9, 3 to 8 and so on.

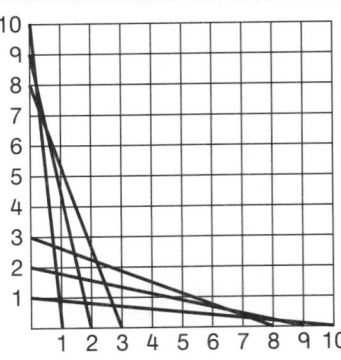

- What if the grid was like this?
- Investigate what other patterns like this you can make.

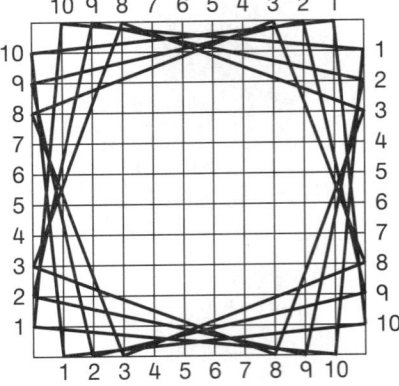

7b Co-ordinates pattern

- squared paper
- ruler
- pencil

- Draw this four quadrant co-ordinates grid on squared paper.
- Join (1, 0) to (0, 10); (1, 0) to (0, -10); (-1, 0) to (0, 10); (-1, 0) to (0, -10).
- Join (2, 0) to (0, 9); (2, 0) to (0, -9); (-2, 0) to (0, 9); (-2, 0) to (0, -9).
- Join (3, 0) to (0, 8); (3, 0) to (0, -8); (-3, 0) to (0, 8); (-3, 0) to (0, -8).
- Continue the pattern.

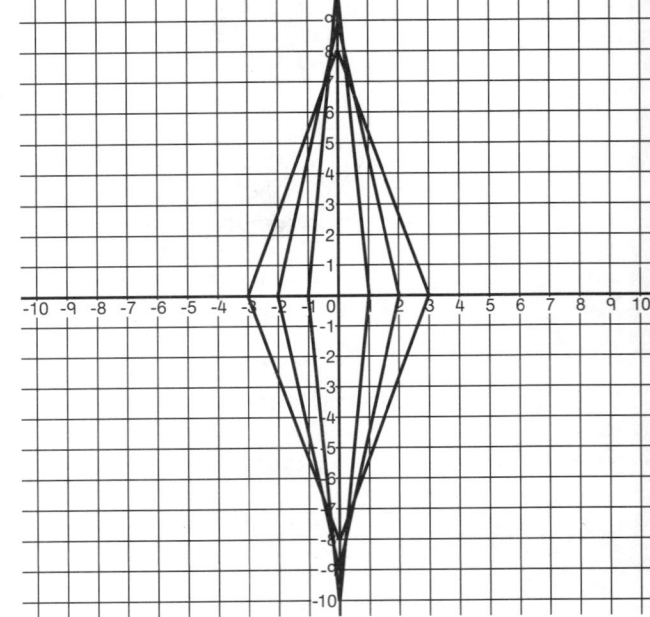

- What other patterns can you make using a four quadrant co-ordinates grid?

7c Circular pattern

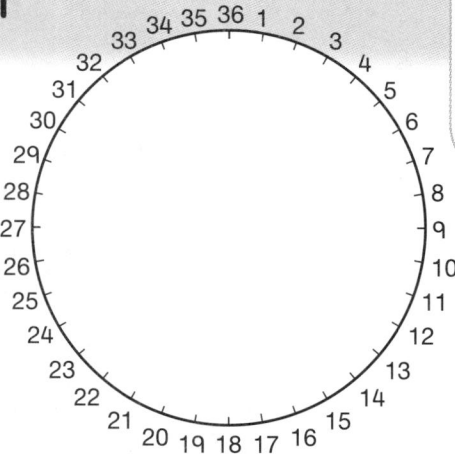

- circular protractor
- ruler
- pencil and paper

- Draw a circle.
- Using a circular protractor, make intervals every 10°.
- Number the points 1 to 36.
- Using a 'multiply by 3' rule, join 1 to 3, 2 to 6, 3 to 9 and so on.

- Investigate what other patterns you can make using a 'multiply by 4' rule, i.e. join 1 to 4, 2 to 8, 3 to 12 and so on.
- What about using a 'multiply by 6' rule, i.e. join 1 to 6, 2 to 12, 3 to 18 and so on?
- What if you used a 'multiply by 2' rule, i.e. join 1 to 2, 2 to 4, 3 to 6 and so on?

7d Shape pattern

- ruler
- protractor
- pencil and paper

- Draw an equilateral triangle with sides 13 cm long.
- Make 1 cm intervals on all three sides of the triangle.
- What different patterns can you make by drawing lines between various intervals on the three sides of the triangle?

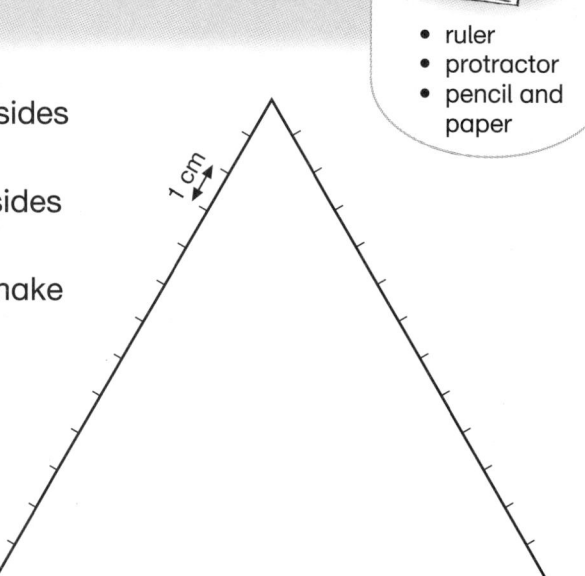

1 cm

- Investigate what patterns you can make using other shapes such as regular hexagons, pentagons and octagons.

8a Letter frequency

• book/novel
• pencil and paper

- Investigate the frequency with which different letters of the alphabet occur in a piece of writing.
- Compare the number of occurrences for each of the 26 letters that make up the English alphabet.
- Are vowels more common than consonants?
- What is the most common letter? What is the least common letter?
- Write the letters in order starting with the most common letter.

- Think about:
  – how many words you are going to 'read' to obtain a reliable sample
  – how you are going to keep a record of the frequency of each letter.

8b Different languages

• book/novel written in English
• book/novel written in another language
• pencil and paper

- Read the first 200 words of a book written in English.
- Read the first 200 words of a book written in another language.
- Investigate the frequency with which different letters of the alphabet occur in different languages.

- How are you going to keep a record of the frequency of each letter?

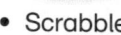
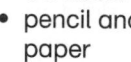

8c Scrabble

- In Scrabble, different values are attached to different letters.
- Investigate the reasoning behind the different values.

- What is the highest scoring word you can make?

8d Morse code

In Morse code, each letter of the alphabet is represented by a sequence of 'dots' and 'dashes'.

A • ▬
B ▬ • • •
C ▬ • ▬ •

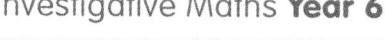

- What are the Morse code sequences for the other letters of the alphabet?
- Investigate the relationship between the number of dots and dashes used for different letters in Morse code and the frequency with which the letters are used.
- As a rule, do the vowels have fewer dots and dashes than the consonants?

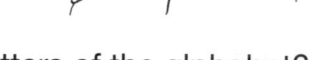

- Use Morse code to send a message to a friend.

9a Cost per kilometre

- travel section of a newspaper
- atlas
- pencil and paper

- Choose 10 places around the world and find the cheapest air fare you can to each of these destinations.
- Now find out how many kilometres it is to each of these destinations.
- Calculate how much it costs you to fly each kilometre to each of these destinations.

- Is there a big difference in the cost per kilometre to different destinations? If so, why do you think this is?

9b Boeing 737

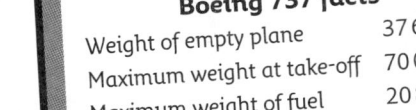

The Boeing 737 is one of the most popular planes for short-haul flights.

Boeing 737 facts

Weight of empty plane	37 648 kg
Maximum weight at take-off	70 080 kg
Maximum weight of fuel	20 894 kg

- pencil and paper

- What is the maximum weight of luggage and people that a Boeing 737 can carry if its fuel tanks are full?
- If there are 148 passengers and 6 crew on board, approximately what is the maximum amount of luggage the plane can carry?
- What is the maximum amount of luggage that each passenger and crew member can have?

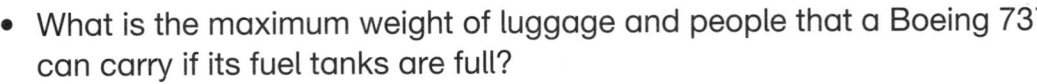

- Think about how you will estimate how much each person weighs.

9c Flying speed

- atlas
- pencil and paper

Speed facts

Boeing 747	567 miles per hour
Boeing 737	530 miles per hour
Airbus A300	547 miles per hour

- Choose a destination in the world to fly to, and find out how far away it is.
- If a Boeing 747, Boeing 737 and Airbus A300 departed at the same time, how far from their destination would the Boeing 737 and the Airbus A300 be when the Boeing 747 was landing?

- Don't forget to use the same units of measurement for both the speed and the distance.

9d How far can they fly?

- atlas
- pencil and paper

	Boeing 747	Boeing 737
Maximum number of litres of fuel plane holds	216840	26022
Number of litres of fuel plane uses per hour	15057	2965
Miles plane travels per hour	567	530

- Work out the maximum distance that the Boeing 747 and Boeing 737 can fly on a full tank of fuel.

- Now find the furthest destination that each plane can fly to, from a UK airport, without refuelling.

10a Cost of light

- packaging from energy saving bulbs
- pencil and paper

150 W bulb costs
0·9p per hour to run.
100 W bulb costs
0·6p per hour to run.
50 W bulb costs
0·3p per hour to run.

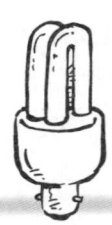  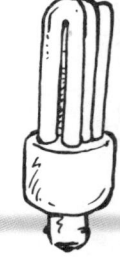

- Investigate how much money you would save in a day if all the bulbs in your house were replaced with energy saving ones.

- What about in a week?

- What about in a year?

- Think about:
  – how powerful the energy saving bulbs need to be to give out the same amount of light as the normal bulbs
  – how long each light is on for each day.

10b Solar power

- electricity bills
- pencil and paper

The cost of solar panels to supply electricity to a household is approximately £6000. These will supply 30% of all the electricity the household needs for free.

- If you installed solar panels where you live, how long would it be before the amount of money you have spent on solar panels equals the amount you have saved in electricity bills?

- If the government gave you a 50% grant for installing solar panels, how long would it be now?

- pencil and paper

10c Travel and trees

Cars are one of the major causes of pollution to our environment.

- Investigate how many kilometres your family car has travelled. (If you have more than one family car investigate this as well.)

- Now work out how many trees need to be grown to absorb the pollution this has caused.

One tree will absorb the pollution generated after driving 5350 km in a small car, 4130 km in a medium car or 3370 km in a large car.

- Have you and your family ever flown on a plane? How many of you went? How far did you travel? How many trees need to be grown to absorb the pollution this caused?

One tree will absorb the pollution caused by one person flying 2900 km.

10d Battery power

Some brands of battery are advertised as lasting longer than other brands.

- different brands of battery all the same size (showing prices)
- battery operated device that uses a lot of power
- measuring equipment
- pencil and paper

- Using the same size of battery, investigate if the cost of a battery is proportional to the length of time it lasts.

- What units of measurement are you going to use to compare the batteries?

11a Fair trade

- pencil and paper

- Investigate whether there is a difference in the price of fair trade food compared to similar products in your local supermarket.

- Be sure to compare products that are as similar as possible and contain the same quantity.

11b Who gets what?

- prices for different pieces of clothing
- pencil and paper

This pie chart shows who gets the money that you pay for an item of clothing produced in the Developing World.

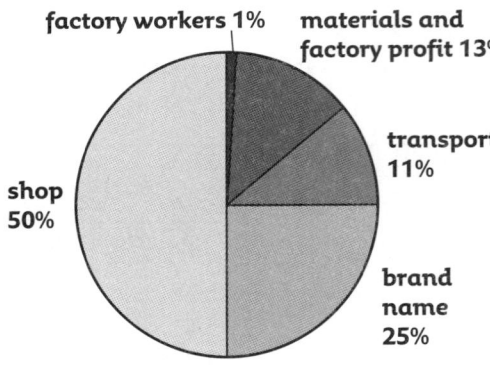

factory workers 1%   materials and factory profit 13%

transport 11%

shop 50%

brand name 25%

- Investigate how much each of the groups in the pie chart gets of the money you paid for an item of your clothing.

- If the average wage in the Developing World is about £5 per week, how many items of your clothing would a factory worker have to make to earn this amount?

11c How many pairs of jeans?

- pencil and paper

The person in the Developing World who makes a pair of jeans that are sold for £37 in a shop in the UK is paid about 37p.

- If you were paid this amount to make a pair of jeans, how many pairs would you have to make to pay for the following:
  - a burger and chips
  - a ticket to the cinema
  - a computer game?

- Think about other things you spend your money on and how many pairs of jeans you would have to make to pay for them.

11d Charities

- pencil and paper

It costs £7 to restore someone's eyesight in the Developing World.

It costs £1.30 to treat a person with malaria.

- Investigate how much it costs to help people in the Developing World in other ways.
- Now work out how much you could help people in the Developing World by donating half the pocket money you get in a year.

- How could your class raise money for a charity in the Developing World?

12a Planning Newtown

- squared paper
- ruler
- coloured pencils
- pencil and paper

- Imagine you are in charge of designing a new town for a population of 10 000 people.

- Give your town a name.

- Draw a map of your town showing which areas are for what use and where the main facilities are.

- Think about:
  - all the facilities your new town will need to have, such as residential areas, shops, schools, hospital...
  - where these facilities will be located
  - how many of your population are children, adults or retired people and how this affects your decisions about the facilities your town has.

12b Redesigning your school

- squared paper
- ruler
- coloured pencils
- pencil and paper

- Imagine your school has been completely demolished.

- Redesign your school, so that it is improved for everyone who uses it.

- Draw to scale a plan of your new school, including measurements.

- Think about:
  - the number of classrooms
  - all the different facilities your school requires.

- Don't forget:
  - your new school must fit on the present site
  - to include the scale.

12c Designing a housing estate

- squared paper
- ruler
- coloured pencils
- pencil and paper

- Imagine you are in charge of designing a new housing estate for 40 homes on a plot of land 170 m by 100 m.
- Draw to scale a plan of your housing estate, including measurements.

- Think about:
  - how big the houses are going to be
  - terraced, semi-detached and/or detached housing
  - roads and pavements
  - individual and/or communal gardens
  - other facilities you would like the estate to have.
- Don't forget to include the scale.

12d New school sports centre

- measuring equipment
- squared paper
- ruler
- coloured pencils
- pencil and paper

- Imagine that your school has been given a plot of land next to it to use as a new playground.
- Your old playground is going to be used to build an indoor sports centre.
- Measure your playground and draw to scale plans for the new sports centre.

- Think about:
  - what facilities you are going to have in your new sports centre
  - how you are going to fit them all in.
- Make sure your new sports centre does not obstruct windows in your school.

13 Multiply, divide and round

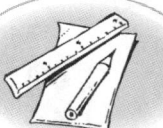

- 1–9 digit cards
- pencil and paper

- Shuffle the 1–9 digit cards and choose the top four cards.

- Use these cards to make as many different 2-, 3- and 4-digit numbers as you can.
- Multiply each of the numbers by 10, 100 and 1000.
- Divide each of the numbers by 10, 100 and 1000.
- Now round every 2-digit number to the nearest 10, 3-digit number to the nearest 10 and 100 and 4-digit number to the nearest 10, 100 and 1000.

- What if you used these cards to make different decimal numbers for tenths, hundredths and thousandths?
- Multiply each of the decimal numbers by 10, 100 and 1000.
- Divide each of the decimal numbers by 10 and 100.
- Now round each decimal with one decimal place to the nearest whole number, each decimal with two decimal places to the nearest whole number and tenth and each decimal with three decimal places to the nearest whole number, tenth and hundredth.

14 Making zero

- -10 to 10 number cards
- pencil and paper

- Shuffle the 21 number cards from -10 to 10.
- Choose the top four cards.
- Using these four numbers, investigate how close to zero you can get using addition and / or subtraction.
- Repeat with other number cards.

- What if you used five number cards?
  Can you make zero in more than one way using the five cards?

15 Adding consecutive numbers

• pencil and paper

- Starting at 1, what is the sum of the first two odd numbers?
- What is the sum of the first three odd numbers?
- What about the sum of the first four odd numbers?
- What do you notice about your answers?
- Can you predict what the sum of the first 8 / 9 / 10 odd numbers are?

- What if you started at 2 and found the sum of the first two even numbers?
- What about the first three / four / five …even numbers?

16 Square numbers

• calculator
• pencil and paper

- What is 1^2?
- What is 11^2?
- What is 111^2?
- What is 1111^2?
- What do you notice?
- Can you predict what $11\,111^2$ is?

- What if you investigated 1^2, 101^2, 1001^2, $10\,001^2$ …?
- What about 3^2, 33^2, 333^2, 3333^2 … / 3^2, 303^2, 3003^2, $30\,003^2$ …?

17 Powers

- calculator
- pencil and paper

A 'power' tells us how many of the same number are multiplied together. 6×6 is shortened to 6^2, where 2 is the power. We say it as '6 to the power of 2' or '6 squared'. $6 \times 6 \times 6$ is shortened to 6^3, where 3 is the power. We say it as '6 to the power of 3'.

$$6^2 = 6 \times 6 = 36$$
$$6^3 = 6 \times 6 \times 6 = 216$$

- Look at the answers to 2^1 to 2^8.
- What pattern do you notice in the units digits?
- What predictions can you make?
- Investigate the answers to 3^1 to 3^8.

$$2^1 = 2$$
$$2^2 = 2 \times 2 = 4$$
$$2^3 = 2 \times 2 \times 2 = 8$$
$$2^4 = 2 \times 2 \times 2 \times 2 = 16$$
$$2^5 = 2 \times 2 \times 2 \times 2 \times 2 = 32$$
$$2^6 = 2 \times 2 \times 2 \times 2 \times 2 \times 2 = 64$$
$$2^7 = 2 \times 2 \times 2 \times 2 \times 2 \times 2 \times 2 = 128$$
$$2^8 = 2 \times 2 \times 2 \times 2 \times 2 \times 2 \times 2 \times 2 = 256$$

- Investigate the answers to 4 / 5 / 6 / 7 … and their powers.

✂ -

18 Triangular numbers

- about 100 counters
- pencil and paper

- Use counters to build a sequence of triangles.

- Use the counters to continue the sequence for 4 more triangles.
- Without using the counters, write the sequence of triangular numbers until you pass 100.
- Can you write the triangular numbers to 300?

- What do you notice about the sum of two consecutive triangular numbers?
- What do you notice about the difference between two consecutive triangular numbers?

19 Proper factors

• pencil and paper

Remember, proper factors of a number are all its factors except 1 and the number itself.

- Investigate which numbers less than 100 have proper factors that are only even numbers.
- Investigate which numbers less than 100 have proper factors that are only odd numbers.

- Investigate which numbers have an even number of proper factors.
- Investigate which numbers have an odd number of proper factors.

1	2	3	4	5	6	7	8	9	10
11	12	13	14	15	16	17	18	19	20
21	22	23	24	25	26	27	28	29	30
31	32	33	34	35	36	37	38	39	40
41	42	43	44	45	46	47	48	49	50
51	52	53	54	55	56	57	58	59	60
61	62	63	64	65	66	67	68	69	70
71	72	73	74	75	76	77	78	79	80
81	82	83	84	85	86	87	88	89	90
91	92	93	94	95	96	97	98	99	100

20 Prime numbers

• squared paper
• coloured pencil
• pencil and paper

- Copy and complete this grid.
- Colour all the prime numbers.
- What do you notice?

1	2	3	4	5
6	7	8	9	10
11	12	13		

- Can you predict how the grid will continue?
- What about this grid? • Or this grid?

1	2	3	4	5	6	7
8	9	10	11	12	13	14
15	16	17				

1	2	3	4	5	6	7
8	9	10	11	12	13	14
15	16	17				

PRIME NUMBER

- What about this grid?
- What about other grids?
- What predictions can you make?

17	18	19		
16	5	6	7	
15	4	1	8	
14	3	2	9	
13	12	11	10	

• pencil and paper

21 Consecutive prime numbers

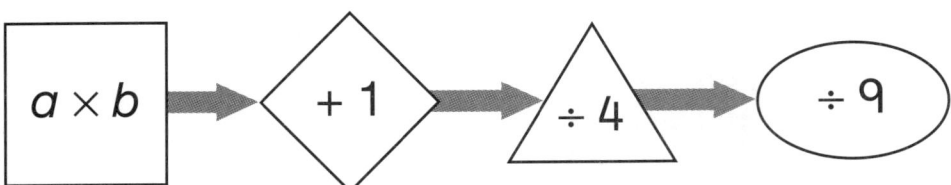

$$a \times b \rightarrow +1 \rightarrow \div 4 \rightarrow \div 9$$

• *a* and *b* are a pair of consecutive prime numbers greater than 3 with a difference of 2.
• Investigate using the flow chart with different values of *a* and *b*.
• What do you notice?

$$a + b + c$$

• *a*, *b* and *c* are 3 consecutive prime numbers greater than 3. Investigate the totals for different values of *a*, *b* and *c*. What do you notice?

© HarperCollins*Publishers* Ltd 2005

---

22 Prime factors

• pencil and paper

20 : 1, 2, 4, 5, 10 and 20

• 20 has two prime factors: 2 and 5.
• Investigate other numbers less than 100 that have 2 prime factors.

• Which numbers have 1, 3 or 4 prime factors?

© HarperCollins*Publishers* Ltd 2005

23 LCM x GCF = ?

• pencil and paper

The product of the lowest common multiple (LCM) and the greatest common factor (GCF) of any two numbers is always equal to the product of those two numbers.

• Do you agree with Emma's statement?

• If you agree with Emma, write a calculation that will work for any pair of numbers.

---

24 Nearer to 1

• pencil and paper

• Choose two digits between 1 and 9.
• Use the digits to make two fractions: a proper fraction and an improper fraction.
• Convert the improper fraction into a mixed number.
• Now calculate the difference between 1 and each of the fractions you have made.
• Which fraction is nearer to 1?
• Do this several times choosing different pairs of digits each time.
• What do you notice?

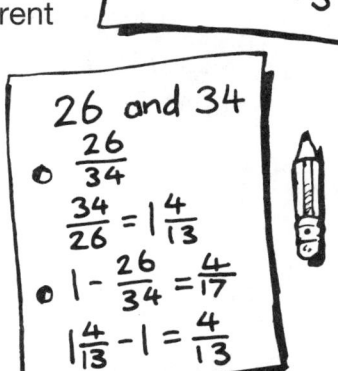

$$3 \text{ and } 7$$
$$\frac{3}{7}$$
$$\frac{7}{3} = 2\frac{1}{3}$$
$$1 - \frac{3}{7} = \frac{4}{7}$$
$$2\frac{1}{3} - 1 = 1\frac{1}{3}$$

$$26 \text{ and } 34$$
$$\frac{26}{34}$$
$$\frac{34}{26} = 1\frac{4}{13}$$
$$1 - \frac{26}{34} = \frac{4}{17}$$
$$1\frac{4}{13} - 1 = \frac{4}{13}$$

• What if you choose a pair of 2-digit numbers?

25 Unitary fractions

A unitary fraction is a fraction that has 1 as its numerator.

- Apart from $\frac{2}{3}$ the Ancient Egyptians only wrote unitary fractions.
- This is how they might have expressed $\frac{3}{4}$ and $\frac{3}{8}$:

$$\frac{3}{4} = \frac{1}{2} + \frac{1}{4} \qquad \frac{3}{8} = \frac{1}{4} + \frac{1}{8}$$

- What non-unitary fractions can you make using the Ancient Egyptian method?

- How can you make the non-unitary fractions you have created using the fewest possible number of fractions?

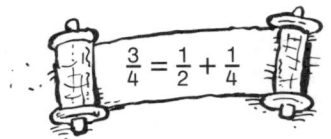

$$\frac{3}{4} = \frac{1}{2} + \frac{1}{4}$$

rather than

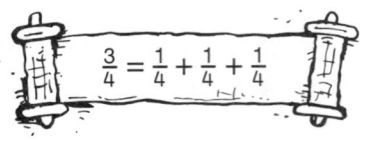

$$\frac{3}{4} = \frac{1}{4} + \frac{1}{4} + \frac{1}{4}$$

---

26 Fractions and decimals

A unitary fraction is a fraction that has 1 as its numerator.

- Convert some unitary fractions into decimals.
- Now sort the decimals into those that have:
  - just one digit to the right of the decimal point, i.e. tenths
  - two digits to the right of the decimal point, i.e. tenths and hundredths
  - three digits to the right of the decimal point, i.e. tenths, hundredths and thousandths
  - recurring decimals, e.g. ·33333...
  - repeating digits, e.g. ·090909...
  - anything different.

- Now try some non-unitary fractions such as $\frac{2}{3}$, $\frac{3}{4}$, $\frac{2}{5}$, $\frac{3}{5}$, $\frac{4}{5}$, $\frac{3}{6}$ ...

27 Percentages

- 0–9 digit cards
- %, × and = cards
- 2 decimal point cards
- pencil and paper

0 1 2 3 4 5 6
7 8 9 $\%$ $\times$ $=$

$$25\% \times 16 = 4$$
$$12\% \times 50 = 6$$

- Using some or all of the 0–9 digit cards and the %, × and = cards, how many different statements can you make?

- What if you included two decimal point cards?

0 1 2 3 4 5 6 7 8 9
$\%$ $\times$ $=$ $\cdot$ $\cdot$

$$2 \cdot 5\% \times 40 = 1$$
$$12 \cdot 5\% \times 64 = 8$$

---

28 Dominoes

- set of dominoes with the double blank removed
- pencil and paper

- Look at a set of dominoes with the double blank removed.
- Count the total number of dots on each domino.  $4 + 3 = 7$
    - What is the ratio of even totals to odd totals?
    - What proportion of the totals is odd?
    - What proportion of the totals is even?

- What if you multiplied together the number of dots on each side?

$4 \times 3 = 12$

    - What is the ratio of even products to odd products?
    - What proportion of the products is odd?
    - What proportion of the products is even?
- What if you found the difference between the number of dots on each side?

$4 - 3 = 1$

• pencil and paper

29 Making even numbers

• Investigate making even numbers from 10 to 50 as the sum of two prime numbers.
• Which even numbers can be written in more than one way as the sum of two prime numbers?

• What about writing even numbers from 10 to 50 as the difference between two prime numbers?
• What if you investigated numbers greater than 50?

30 Between 200 and 300

• pencil and paper

• Use all the digits 0–9 to make a calculation with an answer between 200 and 300.
• Make as many different calculations as you can.

$34 + 75 + 89 + 12 + 60 = 270$

$546 + 18 + 90 - 372 = 282$

$325.6 + 18.9 - 70.4 = 274.1$

• What if you had to have an answer between 200 and 250?
• What about between 250 and 275?

31 Decimal calculation patterns

• pencil and paper

- Work out the answers to these calculations:
- What patterns do you notice?
- Now find the difference between consecutive answers.
- What do you notice about these answers?
- Can you predict the answers for these calculations?

```
11·1 + 1·11 =
22·2 + 2·22 =
33·3 + 3·33 =
44·4 + 4·44 =
```

• What about these calculations?

```
111·1 + 1·111 =
222·2 + 2·222 =
333·3 + 3·333 =
444·4 + 4·444 =
```

```
111·11 + 11·111 =
222·22 + 22·222 =
333·33 + 33·333 =
444·44 + 44·444 =
```

- What if you worked out the answers to these calculations then found the difference between consecutive answers?

```
11·1 - 1·11 =
22·2 - 2·22 =
33·3 - 3·33 =
44·4 - 4·44 =
```

```
111·1 - 1·111 =
222·2 - 2·222 =
333·3 - 3·333 =
444·4 - 4·444 =
```

```
111·11 - 11·111 =
222·22 - 22·222 =
333·33 - 33·333 =
444·44 - 44·444 =
```

32 Letter calculations

• pencil and paper

- In each of these calculations, each letter represents a different digit.
- Work out which digit each letter represents and complete the calculations.

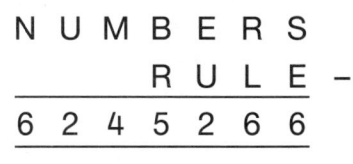

```
  T H I S
    I S
M A T H S  +
4 8 8 6 1
```

```
N U M B E R S
    R U L E  -
6 2 4 5 2 6 6
```

```
  S E N D
  M O R E  +
M O N E Y
```

```
  T E N
  T E N
F O R T Y  +
S I X T Y
```

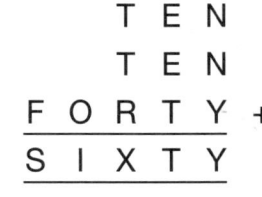

- Make some calculations like these for a friend to solve.

• pencil and paper

33 Number puzzles

• Using each of the digits 1 to 9 once only, write one digit in each of the 9 squares to make the calculations correct.

• Using each of the digits 1 to 9 once only, write one digit in each square so that each line vertically, horizontally and diagonally has the same total.

• Using each of the numbers 1 to 16 once only, write one number in each square so that each line vertically, horizontally and diagonally has the same total.
• Can you do this in more than one way?
• Can you make a puzzle like these for a friend to solve?

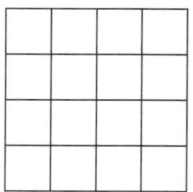

• pencil and paper

34 Making magic squares

This is a magic square.
The sum of each column, row and diagonal is the same – this is the magic number.

8	16	9
12	11	10
13	6	14

• What is the magic number for this magic square?

• Investigate making magic squares using different values for *a*, *b* and *c*.
• What is the magic number for each square you make?

$a - c$	$a + b + c$	$a - b$
$a - b + c$	a	$a + b - c$
$a + b$	$a - b - c$	$a + c$

• Make a magic square where the magic number is 18.

35 Interesting decimals

• pencil and paper

$$0.576$$
$$0.423 \quad 0.103 \quad 0.639 \quad 0.192$$

- Write a decimal less than one with three decimal places.
- Reverse the digits to the right of the decimal point.
- Find the difference.
- Reverse the digits to the right of the decimal point in the answer.
- Add this new number to the answer.
- Try other decimals less than one with three decimal places.
- What do you notice?

- What if the decimals were between 1 and 10, each with 4 digits?

$$8.366$$
$$1.234 \quad 2.159 \quad 5.041$$
$$8.888$$

---

36 Multiplication pairs

• pencil and paper

- What do you notice about the numbers that make up this pair of multiplication calculations?

$$63 \times 24$$
$$36 \times 42$$

- Work out the answer for each calculation.
- What do you notice?
- Can you find other pairs of 2-digit multiplications that do the same thing?

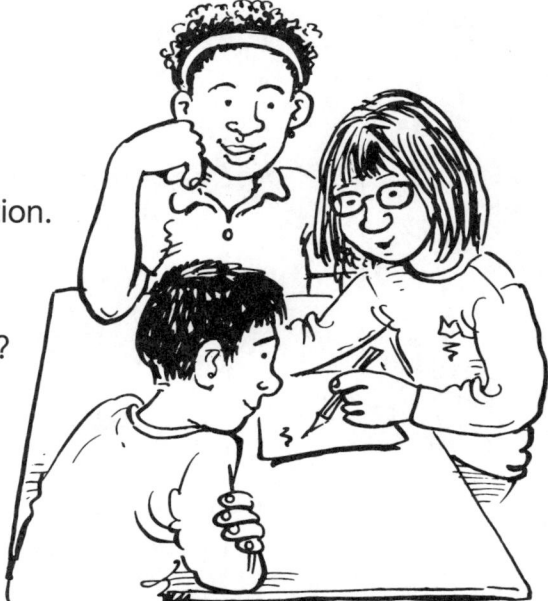

- What if you investigated 3-digit multiplication pairs?

37 Multiplication cards

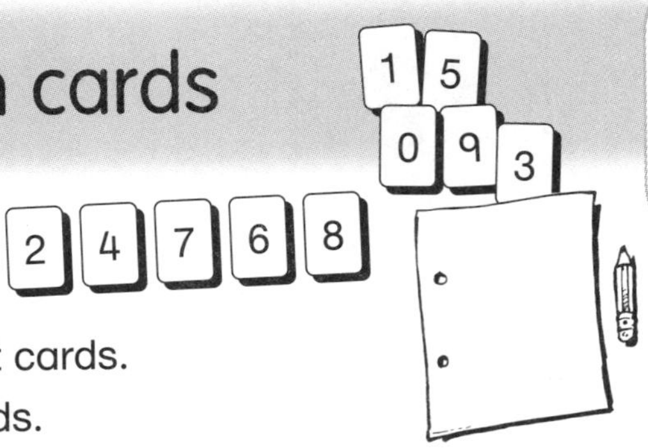

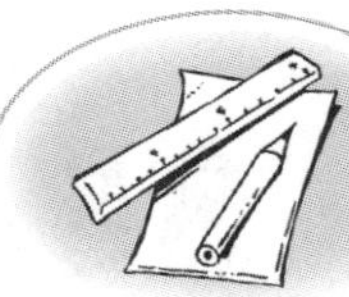

- 0–9 digit cards
- pencil and paper

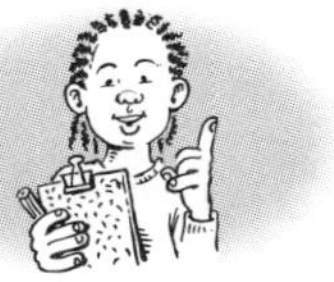

- Shuffle a set of 0–9 digit cards.
- Choose the top five cards.
- Use these five digits to make a 3-digit by 2-digit multiplication calculation:

$$\square\square\square \times \square\square =$$

- Investigate different 3-digit by 2-digit calculations using the same digits.
- Which calculation gives the largest product?
- Which calculation gives the smallest product?
- Can you make a calculation that gives you a product of 30 000?

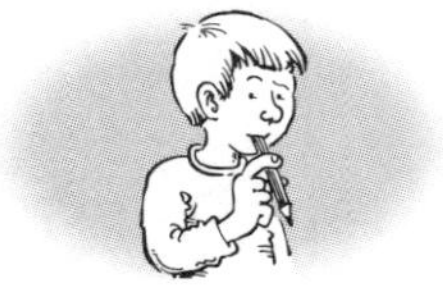

- What if the calculation was 4-digit by 1-digit?

$$\square\square\square\square \times \square =$$

38 Dice calculations

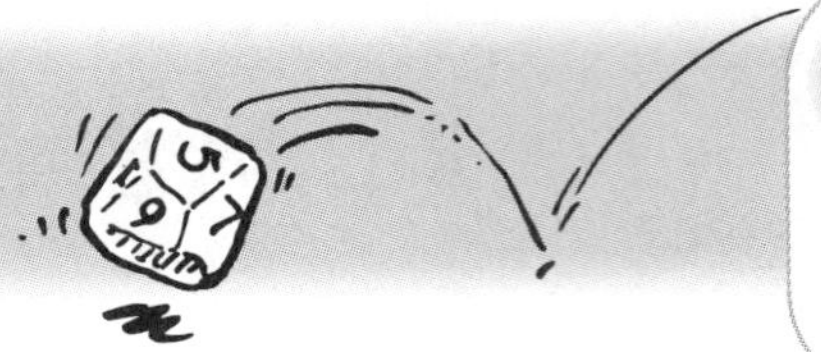

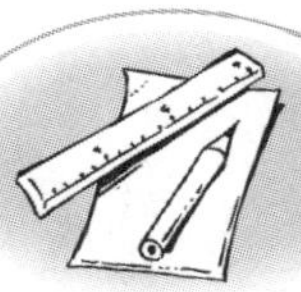

- 0–9 die
- pencil and paper

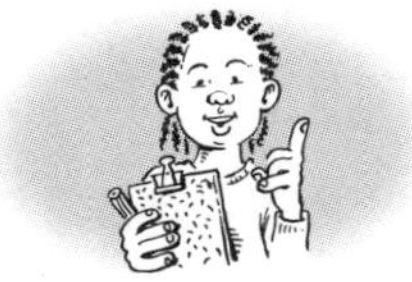

- Roll a 0–9 die four times and write down the numbers.
- Use the four numbers to complete the following calculation:

$$\square . \square\square \times \square =$$

- What is the largest product you can make?
- What is the smallest product you can make?
- Can you use the numbers rolled to make a product of 30? How close to 30 can you get?

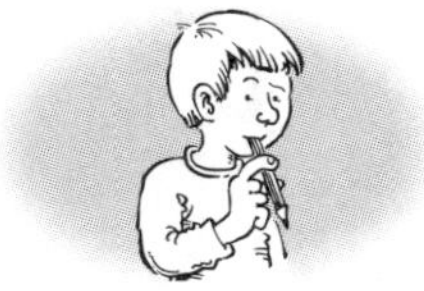

- What if you used the four numbers rolled to complete this calculation:

$$\square\square . \square \div \square =$$

- Can you use the numbers rolled to make an answer of 12? How close to 12 can you get?
- What if you rolled the die five times to complete this calculation:

$$\square . \square\square \times \square\square =$$

- Can you use the numbers rolled to make a product of 300? How close to 300 can you get?

• pencil and paper

39 Algebraic expressions

• If $a = 5$, $b = 3$ and $c = 9$, investigate what answers you get from the following algebraic expressions.

$a + (b - c)$

$a + b + c$

$(a + b) - c$

$a - (b + c)$

$(a - b) + c$

• Now choose some numbers of your own.

• What if the expressions were these?

$a \times (b - c)$

$(a - b) \times c$

$(a + b) \times c$

$(a \times b) - c$

$(a \times b) + c$

• Make up some other expressions using a, b and c.

---

40 Adding squares

• pencil and paper

• Choose a 2-digit number.
• Square each digit and add the answers.
• Keep doing this until the answer is a single digit.
• Investigate doing this for different 2-digit numbers.
• Group them into those that take 1 step, 2 steps, 3 steps and more than 3 steps.

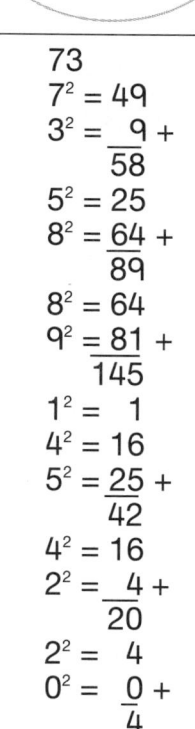

$$
\begin{array}{l}
73 \\
7^2 = 49 \\
3^2 = \underline{9} + \\
 58 \\
5^2 = 25 \\
8^2 = \underline{64} + \\
 89 \\
8^2 = 64 \\
9^2 = \underline{81} + \\
 145 \\
1^2 = 1 \\
4^2 = 16 \\
5^2 = \underline{25} + \\
 42 \\
4^2 = 16 \\
2^2 = \underline{4} + \\
 20 \\
2^2 = 4 \\
0^2 = \underline{0} + \\
 4
\end{array}
$$

• What if you found the difference between the answers?
• What if you started with 3-digit numbers?

• pencil and paper

41 Consecutive odd numbers

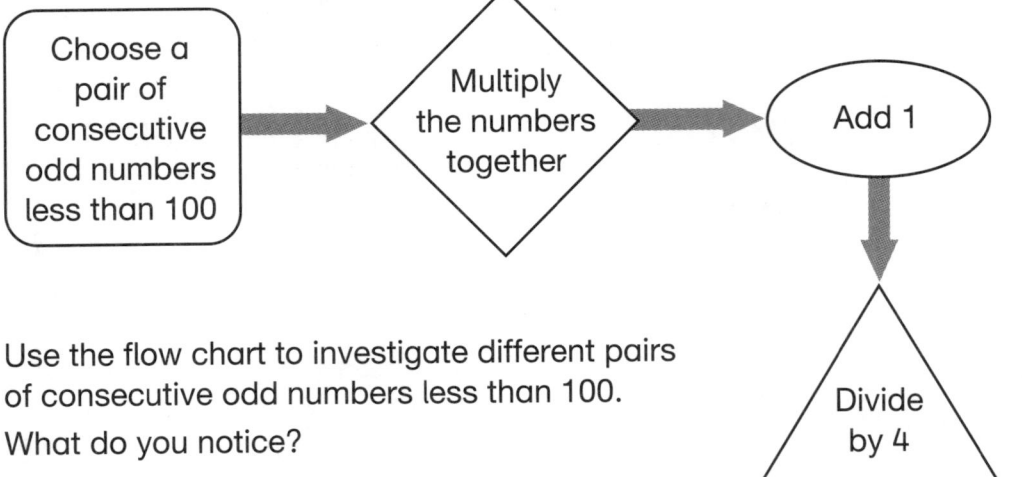

Choose a pair of consecutive odd numbers less than 100 → Multiply the numbers together → Add 1 → Divide by 4

- Use the flow chart to investigate different pairs of consecutive odd numbers less than 100.
- What do you notice?

- What if you investigated different pairs of consecutive odd numbers greater than 100?

• pencil and paper

42 1, 2, 5 and 8

- Using only the digits 1, 2, 5 and 8, investigate writing calculations that give as answers all the numbers from 0 to 10.

RULES:
- All four digits must be used in the calculation.
- Each digit can only be used once in each calculation.
- Digits can be joined together to form 2-digit numbers.
- Use any of the four operations: +, −, × and ÷.
- Brackets are allowed.

- What if you used the digits to make the numbers 11 to 20? What about up to 50 or 100?

43 Currency calculator

- Investigate the exchange rates for the pound against the following currencies:
  - Euro
  - American dollar
  - Maltese Lira.
- Calculate the value of £100 and, using graph paper, draw a conversion graph for each of these currencies.
- Now, using drawing pins and wool or string, make a currency calculator that you can use to change pounds into these currencies as their exchange rates change over time.

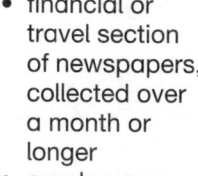

- Can you use your currency calculator to convert pounds into other currencies? Which currencies?
- Which currencies can you not use it for?

---

44 VAT

- Choose some items in a magazine or catalogue that do not have VAT added.
- Calculate the new price of each item once VAT has been added.
- How much money does this add to the cost of each item?

- Choose some items in a magazine or catalogue that already have VAT added.
- Calculate the price of each item before VAT was added.
- How much cheaper is each item without VAT added?

• pencil and paper

45 Coins worth

I'm a 5p coin. I'm worth:

- 5 times as much as a 1p coin
- $2\frac{1}{2}$ times as much as a 2p coin
- $\frac{1}{2}$ of a 10p coin
- $\frac{1}{4}$ of a 20p coin
- $\frac{1}{10}$ of a 50p coin

- $\frac{1}{20}$ of a £1 coin
- $\frac{1}{40}$ of a £2 coin
- $\frac{1}{100}$ as much as a £5 note
- $\frac{1}{200}$ as much as a £10 note
- $\frac{1}{400}$ as much as a £20 note
- $\frac{1}{1000}$ as much as a £50 note

- Investigate how much each coin and note is worth in relation to all the other coins and notes.
- Write your answers as fractions.

- What if you wrote your answers as decimals?

---

46 Where are they?

• pencil and paper

- Four children are sitting at a table.
- They each follow a different football team: Arsenal, Manchester United, Liverpool or Chelsea.
- Read the clues to find out where each child is sitting and which football team they support.
- Each person is facing the table.

Sarah is sitting between someone who supports Arsenal and someone who supports Manchester United.

Lisa is across the table from someone who supports Liverpool.

The Arsenal supporter is sitting across from Annie.

Kylie is sitting on the left of the Liverpool supporter.

- Make up a problem like this for a friend to solve. Try and make it as tricky as you can.

47 Sorting cards

- pack of playing cards without K, Q, J or joker
- pencil and paper

- Investigate the probabilities of taking different kinds of cards from the pack.
- Predict and record the probability of choosing from the pack:
  - a red card
  - a heart
  - an odd number.

- What is the probability of choosing a black card / a club / an even number?
- What is the probability of choosing a red number 10 card?
- What about a spade with an even number?
- What if you included the K, Q and J?

48 Handling dice data

- two 0–9 dice
- pencil and paper

- Roll two 0–9 dice 30 times.
- After each roll of the dice write down the two numbers rolled.
- Work out the total for each pair of numbers.
- Investigate the mode, range, median and mean of the 30 totals.

6, 3 (9)
8, 2 (10)
4, 4 (8)
5, 1 (6)

- What if you found the difference between each pair of numbers?

6, 3 (3)
8, 2 (6)
4, 4 (0)
5, 1 (4)

- What if you found the product of each pair of numbers?

6, 3 (18)
8, 2 (16)
4, 4 (16)
5, 1 (5)

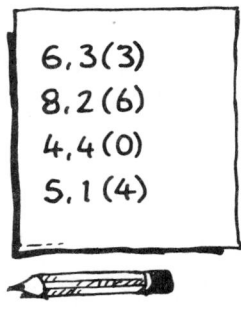

49 Metric and imperial measures

- various classroom objects to measure
- measuring equipment (metric and imperial)
- pencil and paper

- Measure the length, mass and/or capacity of the objects collected, using metric measures.
- Use this table to convert the metric measures to imperial measures.

Conversion Table		
Multiply	by	to obtain
millimetres	0·03937	inches
centimetres	0·3937	inches
metre	3·281	feet
metre	1·0936	yards
kilometres	0·6214	miles
grams	0·0352	ounces
kilograms	2·2046	pounds
millilitres	0·035	ounces
litres	2·1	pints
litres	0·22	gallons

- Now collect some different objects to measure.
- This time measure the length, mass and/or capacity of the objects using imperial measures.
- Use this table to convert the imperial measures to metric measures.

Conversion Table		
Multiply	by	to obtain
inches	25·4	millimetres
feet	30·48	centimetres
yards	0·9144	metres
miles	1·609	kilometres
ounces	28·41	grams
pounds	0·4536	kilograms
ounces	28·41	millilitres
pints	0·568	litres
gallons	4·54	litres

50 Temperature

- newspaper
- pencil and paper

Temperature is either measured in degrees Celsius (°C) or degrees Fahrenheit (°F).

To convert Celsius to Fahrenheit
$(\frac{9}{5} \times °C) + 32$

To convert Fahrenheit to Celsius
$(\frac{5}{9} \times °F) - 32$

- Look for the temperature guide in the weather section of a newspaper.
- Convert the temperatures in the newspaper from Celsius to Fahrenheit or from Fahrenheit to Celsius using the temperature conversions above.

- Draw a table to show the temperature in degrees Celsius for various different temperatures in degrees Fahrenheit.

51 Dan's van

• pencil and paper

- Dan's van can carry a maximum load of 1·4 tonnes.

- His load compartment is 1·7 metres wide, 1·85 metres high and 4·2 metres long.

- Below is a list of items that Dan has to deliver to a department store.

Item	Quantity	Weight	Dimensions (W × H × D)
Small fridge	15	20 kg each	545 mm × 1346 mm × 600 mm
Slimline dishwasher	30	25 kg each	45 cm × 85 cm × 58 cm
Washing machine	25	50 kg each	495 mm × 670 mm × 515 mm
Gas cooker	15	30 kg each	0·6 m × 0·9 cm × 0·6 cm
LCD TV	100	4·8 kg each	55 cm × 47 cm × 22 cm
DVD Video Player	115	3 kg each	45 cm × 8 cm × 32 cm

- Which items should Dan choose to put in each load so that he makes the fewest number of deliveries?

- What if Dan's van could carry a maximum load of 1·2 tonnes and his freight compartment was 2·1 metres wide, 2·1 metres high and 3 metres long?

---

52 Time differences

• pencil and paper

- Investigate the time difference between London and the other cities on the map.

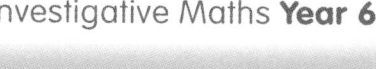

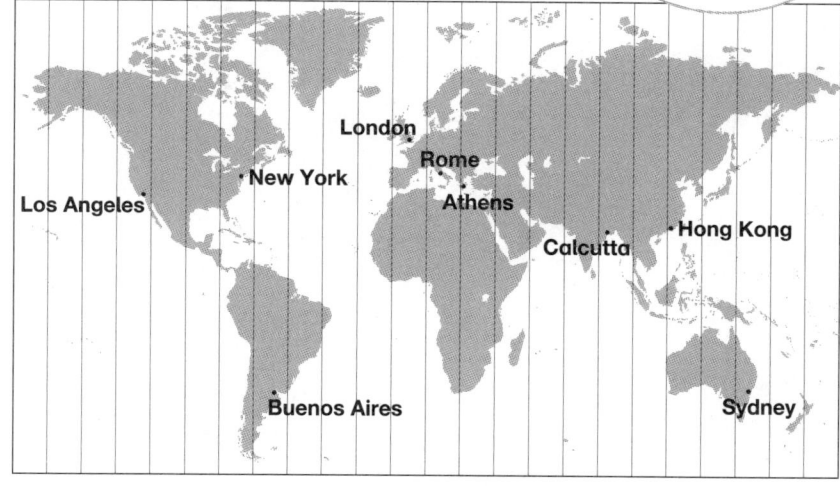

- Investigate what time it would be in each of the other 8 cities if it were:
  - 05:00 in London
  - 09:30 in New York
  - 14:00 in Hong Kong
  - 16:00 in Rome
  - 12:00 in Los Angeles
  - 23:00 in Calcutta
  - 22:00 in Athens
  - 06:30 in Buenos Aires
  - 17:30 in Sydney.

- pencil and paper

53 Field measurements

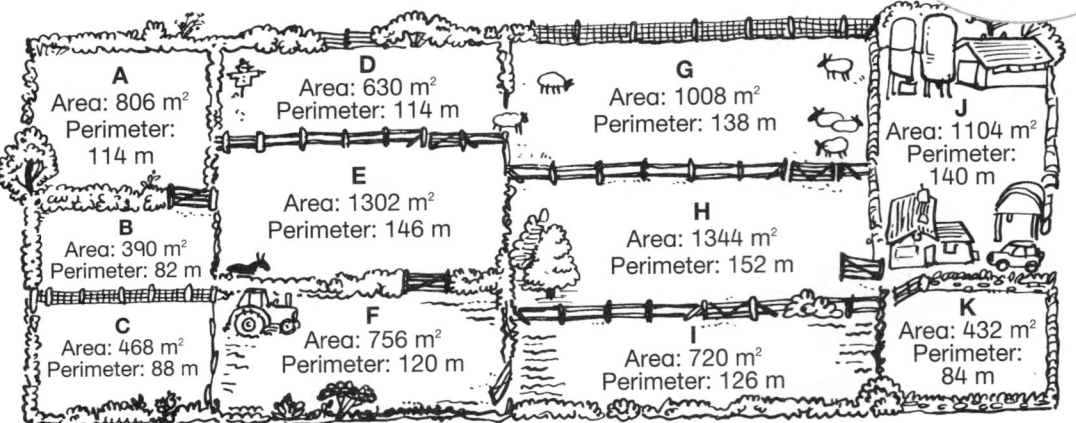

A
Area: 806 m²
Perimeter: 114 m

D
Area: 630 m²
Perimeter: 114 m

G
Area: 1008 m²
Perimeter: 138 m

J
Area: 1104 m²
Perimeter: 140 m

B
Area: 390 m²
Perimeter: 82 m

E
Area: 1302 m²
Perimeter: 146 m

H
Area: 1344 m²
Perimeter: 152 m

C
Area: 468 m²
Perimeter: 88 m

F
Area: 756 m²
Perimeter: 120 m

I
Area: 720 m²
Perimeter: 126 m

K
Area: 432 m²
Perimeter: 84 m

- A farmer calculated the area and perimeter of all the fields on his farm.
- Use this information to calculate the dimensions of each field.

- Given the total area of the farm and the same number of fields, what other sizes could the fields be?

✂

54 Triangular areas

- dotty squared paper
- ruler
- pencil and paper

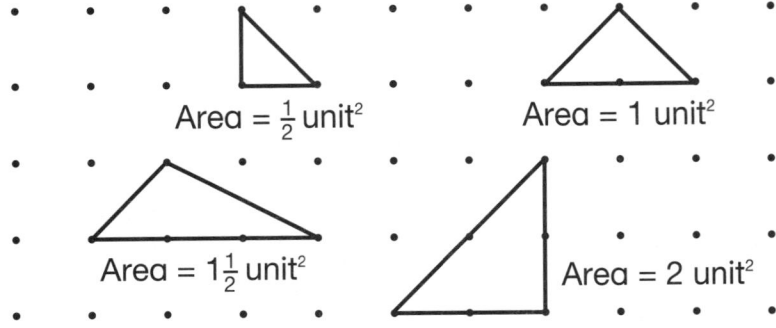

Area = $\frac{1}{2}$ unit²

Area = 1 unit²

Area = $1\frac{1}{2}$ unit²

Area = 2 unit²

- These four triangles show areas of $\frac{1}{2}$ unit², 1 unit², $1\frac{1}{2}$ unit² and 2 unit².
- Investigate drawing triangles with an area of $2\frac{1}{2}$ unit², 3 unit², $3\frac{1}{2}$ unit², 4 unit²…

- Investigate different ways of drawing triangles with an area of $\frac{1}{2}$ unit², 1 unit², $1\frac{1}{2}$ unit², 2 unit², $2\frac{1}{2}$ unit², 3 unit²…

55 Area of a circle

I used this method to work out the area of a circle.

- squared paper
- ruler
- pencil and paper

Step 1
Draw a circle.

Step 2
Draw a square around the circle.

Step 3
Divide the square into smaller squares.

Step 4
Divide the four corner squares in half to make an octagon.

Step 5
Calculate the area of the octagon as an approximation of the area of the circle.

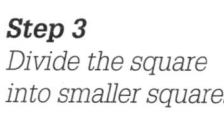

- Investigate Jake's method for finding the area of different circles.

- How else might you measure the area of a circle?

---

56 Polygon designs

- squared paper
- ruler
- coloured pencils
- pencil and paper

This is a pentagram. It is made by drawing all the diagonals of a regular pentagon. The regions can be coloured to create a design.

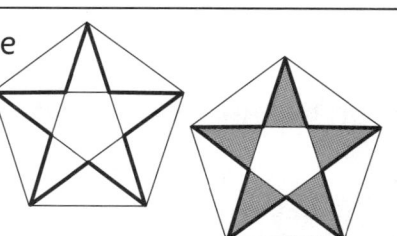

- Create your own pentagram designs using one coloured pencil.
- You can add other lines to help you create a more elaborate design.

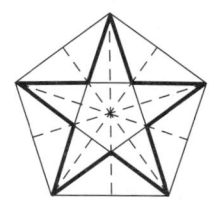

- What if you used two or more coloured pencils?
- What about creating a hexagram design or an octagram design?

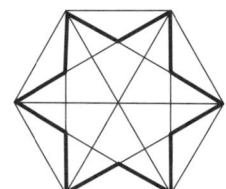 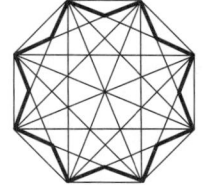

57 Translating shapes

- dotty squared paper
- pencil and paper

- On a 2 × 2 grid there is one possible translation of a 1 × 2 rectangle.

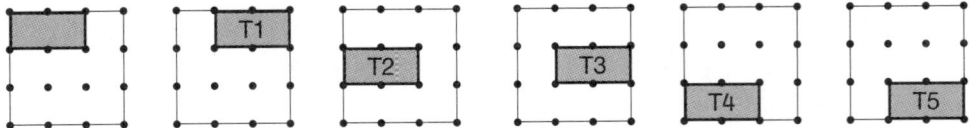

- On a 3 × 3 grid there are five possible translations of a 1 × 2 rectangle.

- Investigate possible translations of the rectangle on a 4 × 4 grid.
- Can you predict how many possible translations there would be on a 5 × 5 grid?

- What if the rectangle was a different shape?

---

58 Reflect, translate, rotate

- centimetre squared paper
- coloured pencils
- pencil and paper

Simple shapes can be made into a design by:

Reflection

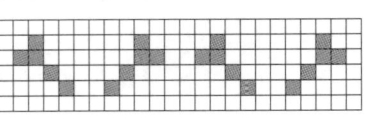

Translation

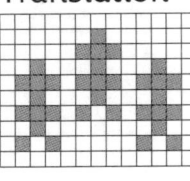

Rotation

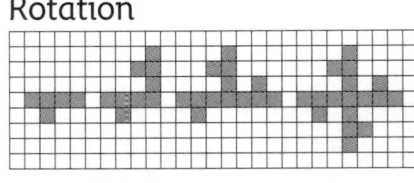

- Using squared paper and one coloured pencil, make your own design using reflection, translation and rotation.

- What if you used two or more coloured pencils to make your design?

59 Co-ordinating shapes

- centimetre squared paper
- pencil and paper

- Draw a polygon so that it has at least one vertex in each of the four quadrants of the grid.
- Write down the co-ordinates of your shape.
- Reverse the signs for the co-ordinates.
- Now draw a shape using these co-ordinates.
- Investigate doing this for other polygons.

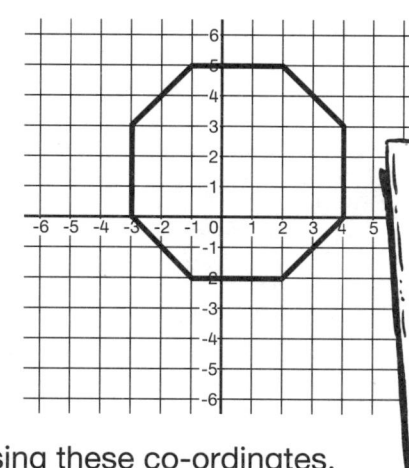

(2,5), (-1,5), (-3,3),
(-3,0), (-1,-2), (2,-2),
(4,0), (4,3), (-2,-5),
(1,-5), (3,-3), (3,0),
(1,

- Using only the digits 2, 3, 5 and 6, make different co-ordinates, e.g. (-3, 5), (-2, –3), (2, 3) or (6, -5). Using these co-ordinates what shapes can you make?

---

60 Angle shapes

I used this method to calculate the sum of angles in a regular pentagon.

- squared paper
- ruler
- protractor
- pencil and paper

Step 1	**Step 2**	**Step 3**	**Step 4**
Draw a regular pentagon.	*Choose any vertex of the pentagon and connect it to all the other vertices.*	*Count the number of triangles.* 3	*Multiply the number of triangles by 180° (the number of degrees in a triangle).* 3 × 180° = 540°

- Investigate Naomi's method for calculating the sum of angles in other regular polygons.

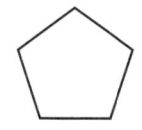

- If *n* represents the number of sides of a polygon and the number of triangles that can be made is *n* – 2, investigate this formula for calculating the sum of interior angles.

$$180 \times (n - 2)$$

Answers

Please note not all activities have answers.

Activity 13

Using 4 digit cards it is possible to make:
- 12 different 2-digit numbers
- 24 different 3-digit numbers
- 24 different 4-digit numbers.

Activity 15

The answers are all square numbers.

$1 + 3 = 4 \ (2^2)$

$1 + 3 + 5 = 9 \ (3^2)$

$1 + 3 + 5 + 7 = 16 \ (4^2)$

⋮

⋮

$1 + 3 + 5 + 7 + 9 + 11 + 13 + 15 = 64 \ (8^2)$

$1 + 3 + 5 + 7 + 9 + 11 + 13 + 15 + 17 = 81 \ (9^2)$

$1 + 3 + 5 + 7 + 9 + 11 + 13 + 15 + 17 + 19 = 100 \ (10^2)$

Activity 16

$1^2 = 1$

$11^2 = 121$

$111^2 = 12\,321$

$1111^2 = 1\,234\,321$

$11\,111^2 = 1\,2345\,4321$

Activity 17

The units digits in the answers to the powers of 2 form a repeating pattern: 2, 4, 8, 6, 2, 4, 8, 6…

The units digits in the answers to the powers of 3 form a repeating pattern: 9, 7, 1, 3, 9, 7, 1, 3…

Activity 18

The triangular numbers from 1 to 300 are: 1, 3, 6, 10, 15, 21, 28, 36, 45, 55, 66, 78, 91, 105, 120, 136, 153, 171, 190, 210, 231, 253, 276 and 300.

Activity 19

Numbers less than 100 that have proper factors that are only even numbers: 4, 8, 16, 32 and 64.

Numbers less than 100 that have proper factors that are only odd numbers: 9, 15, 21, 25, 27, 33, 35, 39, 45, 49, 51, 55, 57, 63, 65, 69, 75, 77, 81, 85, 87, 91, 93, 95 and 99.

Activity 20

Accept any patterns that the children notice about each grid.

Activity 21

The answer is always a square number.

Activity 22

There are 52 numbers less than 100 that have two prime factors:

6: 2 and 3	34: 2 and 17
10: 2 and 5	35: 5 and 7
12: 2 and 3	36: 2 and 3
14: 2 and 7	38: 2 and 19
15: 3 and 5	39: 3 and 19
18: 2 and 3	40: 2 and 5
20: 2 and 5	44: 2 and 11
21: 3 and 7	45: 3 and 5
22: 2 and 11	46: 2 and 23
24: 2 and 3	48: 2 and 3
26: 2 and 13	50: 2 and 5
28: 2 and 7	51: 3 and 17
33: 3 and 11	52: 2 and 13
54: 2 and 3	85: 5 and 17
55: 5 and 11	86: 2 and 43
56: 2 and 7	87: 3 and 29
57: 3 and 19	88: 2 and 11
58: 2 and 29	91: 7 and 13
62: 2 and 31	92: 2 and 23
63: 3 and 7	93: 3 and 31
65: 5 and 13	94: 2 and 47
69: 3 and 23	95: 5 and 19
72: 2 and 3	96: 2 and 3
74: 2 and 37	98: 2 and 7
77: 7 and 11	99: 3 and 11
82: 2 and 41	100: 2 and 5

Activity 23

Emma's statement is correct. The product of the lowest common multiple (LCM) and greatest common factor (GCF) of any two numbers is always equal to the product of those two numbers. For example, 6 and 9: The LCM is 18, the GCF is 3. 18 × 3 is equal to 6 × 9.

Activity 24

Whichever digits are chosen, the proper fraction is always nearer to 1 than the improper fraction.

Activity 25

Accept any calculations that involve unitary fractions where the answer is not a unitary fraction, e.g.

$\frac{1}{2} + \frac{1}{4} = \frac{3}{4}$ $\frac{1}{5} + \frac{1}{5} = \frac{2}{5}$

Activity 26

The following shows the fractions and their decimal equivalents from $\frac{1}{2}$ to $\frac{1}{15}$.

Tenths: $\frac{1}{2}$ (0·5), $\frac{1}{5}$ (0·2) and $\frac{1}{10}$ (0·1)

Tenths and hundredths: $\frac{1}{4}$ (0·25)

Tenths, hundredths and thousandths: $\frac{1}{8}$ (0·125)

Recurring decimals:
$\frac{1}{3}$ (0·3̇3̇), $\frac{1}{6}$ (0·166̇) $\frac{1}{9}$ (0·1̇1̇),
$\frac{1}{12}$ (0·0833̇) and $\frac{1}{15}$ (0·066̇)

Repeating digits: $\frac{1}{11}$ (0·090909...)

Anything different: $\frac{1}{7}$ (0·1428571),
$\frac{1}{13}$ (0·076923) and $\frac{1}{14}$ (0·0714285)

Activity 28

Ratio of even totals to odd totals:
5 : 4

Proportion of the odd totals: $\frac{5}{9}$
Proportion of the even totals: $\frac{4}{9}$

Activity 29

10 = 5 + 5, 7 + 3
12 = 7 + 5
14 = 11 + 3, 7 + 7
16 = 11 + 5, 13 + 3
18 = 11 + 7, 13 + 5
20 = 17 + 3, 13 + 7
22 = 17 + 5, 19 + 3, 11 + 11
24 = 17 + 7, 19 + 5, 13 + 11
26 = 23 + 3, 19 + 7, 17 + 9,
     13 + 13
28 = 23 + 5, 17 + 11
30 = 23 + 7, 19 + 11
32 = 29 + 3, 19 + 13
34 = 31 + 3, 29 + 5, 23 + 11,
     17 + 17
36 = 31 + 5, 29 + 7, 23 + 13,
     19 + 17
38 = 31 + 7, 19 + 19
40 = 37 + 3, 31 + 9, 29 + 11,
     23 + 17
42 = 37 + 5, 31 + 11
44 = 41 + 3, 37 + 7, 31 + 13
46 = 43 + 3, 41 + 5, 37 + 9,
     29 + 17, 23 + 23
48 = 41 + 7, 43 + 5
50 = 43 + 7, 47 + 3

Activity 31

11·1 + 1·11 = 12·21
22·2 + 2·22 = 24·42
33·3 + 3·33 = 36·63
44·4 + 4·44 = 48·84

In each of the calculations the tens and hundredths digits are the same; and the units and tenths digits are the same. In each successive calculation the tens and hundredths digits increase by one each time; and the units and tenths digits increase by two each time.

The difference between consecutive answers is 12·21: the answer to the first calculation.

111·1 + 1·111 = 112·211
222·2 + 2·222 = 224·422
333·3 + 3·333 = 336·633
444·4 + 4·444 = 448·844

In each successive calculation the hundreds and tens digits increase by one each time, the units and tenths digits increase by 2, and the hundredths and thousandths digits increase by one each time.

The difference between consecutive answers is 112·211: the answer to the first calculation.

111·11 + 11·111 = 122·221
222·22 + 22·222 = 244·442
333·33 + 33·333 = 366·663
444·44 + 44·444 = 488·884

In each successive calculation the hundreds and thousandths digits increase by one each time. The tens, units, tenths and hundredths digits are identical in each calculation and each of them increases by two each time.

The difference between consecutive answers is 122·221: the answer to the first calculation.

Activity 32

```
  5 2 6 7        6 2 5 3 4 8 0
    6 7              8 2 1 4 −
4 3 5 2 7 +      6 2 4 5 2 6 6
4 8 8 6 1
```

More than one answer is possible.

```
9 5 6 7            8 5 0
1 0 8 5 +          8 5 0
1 0 6 5 2        2 9 7 8 6 +
                 3 1 4 8 6
```

Activity 33

$$\boxed{6} \div \boxed{3} = \boxed{2}$$
$$\times$$
$$\boxed{9} - \boxed{5} = \boxed{4}$$
$$=$$
$$\boxed{7} + \boxed{1} = \boxed{8}$$

2	9	4
7	5	3
6	1	8

Other answers are possible.

Activity 34

The magic number is 33.

Activity 35

The answer is always 1·089.

Activity 36

Reversing the digits in the first calculation makes the numbers in the second calculation.

The answer to both calculations is the same: 1512.

Activity 39

$(a + b) - c = (5 + 3) - 9 = -1$
$a + (b - c) = 5 + (3 - 9) = -1$
$a + b + c = 5 + 3 + 9 = 17$
$a - (b + c) = 5 - (3 + 9) = -7$
$(a - b) + c = (5 - 3) + 9 = 11$

Activity 40

1 step: 10, 11, 12, 20, 21,
    22 and 30.
2 steps: 13, 24, 31 and 42.
3 steps: 23 and 32.
More than 3 steps: any 2-digit number not mentioned above.

Activity 41

The answers are square numbers.

Activity 42

0: $8 - 5 - 2 - 1$
1: $(2 \times 5) - (8 + 1)$
2: $(2 \times 5 \times 1) - 8$
3: $(2 \times 5) + 1 - 8$
4: $(8 \times 2) \div (5 - 1)$
5: $(8 \div 1) + 2 - 5$
6: $18 \div (5 - 2)$
7: $28 \div (5 - 1)$
8: $(8 \div 2) + 5 - 1$
9: $(8 \div 2) + (5 \times 1)$
10: $(2 \times 8) - 5 - 1$

Different calculations are possible for each number.

Activity 45

See below

Activity 46

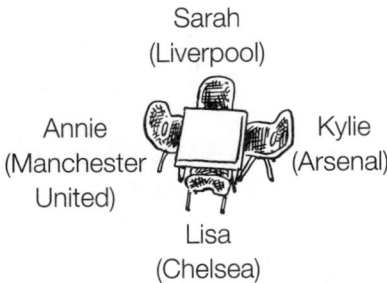

Sarah (Liverpool)

Annie (Manchester United)

Kylie (Arsenal)

Lisa (Chelsea)

Activity 47

The probabilities are as follows:
– red card: 1 in 2
– heart: 1 in 4
– odd number: 1 in 2

Activity 51

The fewest number of deliveries Dan could make is three.

The loads could be split in the following ways:
– 15 Gas cookers and 30 Slimline dishwashers.
– 14 Small fridges, 7 Washing machines, 64 LCD TVs and 15 DVD Video Players.
– 18 Washing machines, 1 Small fridge, 36 LCD TVs and 100 DVD Video Players.

Other answers are possible.

Activity 52

The time difference between London and the following cities is:
– Rome: +1 hour
– Athens: +2 hours
– New York: –5 hours
– Los Angeles: –8 hours
– Buenos Aires: –4 hours
– Hong Kong: +8 hours
– Calcutta: +6 hours
– Sydney: +10 hours

Activity 53

A: 31 m by 26 m
B: 15 m by 26 m
C: 18 m by 26 m
D: 15 m by 42 m
E: 31 m by 42 m
F: 18 m by 42 m
G: 21 m by 48 m
H: 28 m by 48 m
I: 15 m by 48 m
J: 46 m by 24 m
K: 18 m by 24 m

Activity 54

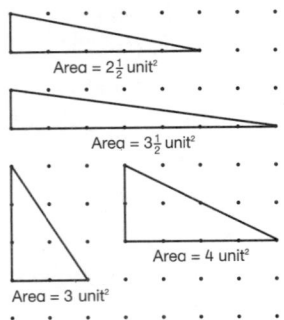

Area = $2\frac{1}{2}$ unit²

Area = $3\frac{1}{2}$ unit²

Area = 4 unit²

Area = 3 unit²

Activity 57

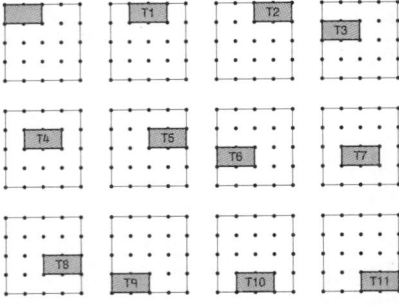

There are 19 possible translations on a 5 × 5 grid.

Activity 60

3-sided shape (triangle): 180°
4-sided shape (square): 360°
5-sided shape (pentagon): 540°
6-sided shape (hexagon): 720°
7-sided shape (heptagon): 900°
8-sided shape (octagon): 1080°
9-sided shape (nonagon): 1260°
10-sided shape (decagon): 1440°
12-sided shape (dodecagon): 1800°

Activity 45

	1p	2p	5p	10p	20p	50p	£1	£2	£5	£10	£20	£50
1p		$\frac{1}{2}$	$\frac{1}{5}$	$\frac{1}{10}$	$\frac{1}{20}$	$\frac{1}{50}$	$\frac{1}{100}$	$\frac{1}{200}$	$\frac{1}{500}$	$\frac{1}{1000}$	$\frac{1}{2000}$	$\frac{1}{5000}$
2p	2×		$\frac{2}{5}$	$\frac{1}{5}$	$\frac{1}{10}$	$\frac{1}{25}$	$\frac{1}{50}$	$\frac{1}{100}$	$\frac{1}{250}$	$\frac{1}{500}$	$\frac{1}{1000}$	$\frac{1}{2500}$
5p	5×	$2\frac{1}{2}$×		$\frac{1}{2}$	$\frac{1}{4}$	$\frac{1}{10}$	$\frac{1}{20}$	$\frac{1}{40}$	$\frac{1}{100}$	$\frac{1}{200}$	$\frac{1}{400}$	$\frac{1}{1000}$
10p	10×	5×	2×		$\frac{1}{2}$	$\frac{1}{5}$	$\frac{1}{10}$	$\frac{1}{20}$	$\frac{1}{50}$	$\frac{1}{100}$	$\frac{1}{200}$	$\frac{1}{500}$
20p	20×	10×	4×	2×		$\frac{2}{5}$	$\frac{1}{5}$	$\frac{1}{10}$	$\frac{1}{25}$	$\frac{1}{50}$	$\frac{1}{100}$	$\frac{1}{250}$
50p	50×	25×	10×	5×	$2\frac{1}{2}$×		$\frac{1}{2}$	$\frac{1}{4}$	$\frac{1}{10}$	$\frac{1}{20}$	$\frac{1}{40}$	$\frac{1}{100}$
£1	100×	50×	20×	10×	5×	2×		$\frac{1}{2}$	$\frac{1}{5}$	$\frac{1}{10}$	$\frac{1}{20}$	$\frac{1}{50}$
£2	200×	100×	40×	20×	10×	5×	2×		$\frac{2}{5}$	$\frac{1}{5}$	$\frac{1}{10}$	$\frac{1}{25}$
£5	500×	250×	100×	50×	25×	10×	5×	$2\frac{1}{2}$×		$\frac{1}{2}$	$\frac{1}{4}$	$\frac{1}{10}$
£10	1000×	500×	200×	100×	50×	20×	10×	5×	2×		$\frac{2}{5}$	$\frac{1}{5}$
£20	2000×	1000×	400×	200×	100×	50×	20×	10×	4×	2×		$\frac{2}{5}$
£50	5000×	2500×	1000×	500×	250×	100×	50×	25×	10×	5×	$2\frac{1}{2}$×	